QUEEN ELIZABETH I
AND HER COURT

QUEEN ELIZABETH I
AND HER COURT

by

Lisa Hopkins

VISION PRESS · LONDON
ST. MARTIN'S PRESS · NEW YORK

Vision Press Ltd.
c/o Vine House Distribution
Waldenbury, North Common
Chailey, E. Sussex BN8 4DR

and

St. Martin's Press, Inc.
175 Fifth Avenue
New York
N.Y. 10010

ISBN (UK) 0 85478 107 2
ISBN (US) 0 312 03568 3

British Library Cataloguing-in-Publication Data

Hopkins (née Cronin), Lisa
    Elizabeth I and her court.
    1. England. Royal Courts. Social life, 1558–
        1603.
    I. Title.
    942.05′5   ISBN 0 85478 107 2

Library of Congress Cataloging-in-Publication Data

Hopkins, Lisa, 1962–
    Elizabeth I and her court/Lisa Hopkins.
    Includes bibliographical references.
    ISBN 0-312-03568-3
    1. Elizabeth I, Queen of England, 1533–1603. 2. Great
Britain—History— Elizabeth, 1558–1603. 3. Great Britain—Court
and courtiers— History—16th century. I. Title.
DA356.H75   1990
94205′5′092—dc20   89-48756
(B)   CIP

For Chris and my parents

Printed and bound in Great Britain by
Billing & Sons, Worcester.
Typeset by Galleon Photosetting,
Ipswich, Suffolk.
MCMLXXXX

Contents

I

Princess Elizabeth

ON the warm, sunny afternoon of Sunday, 7 September 1533, the Queen of England lay in labour at the palace of Greenwich, and the court made excited preparations for the arrival of a prince. Already the carpenters had finished work on a suitably splendid cradle for him—five and a half feet long by two and a half feet wide, bearing the arms of his parents, the King and Queen. It was covered in cloth of gold and crimson, and its scarlet coverlet had an ermine lining and a blue velvet border. Not that the little prince would actually sleep in this: his real cot was a snug forty-five inches long and twenty-two inches wide, although it, too, was painted gold. The larger cradle was only for show, to impress the important visitors and the foreign ambassadors who would want to see the baby so that they could report back to their masters on whether he had any deformities or whether he looked strong and sturdy—whether, like so many babies of the Tudor period, he appeared likely to die young, or whether he looked like living and becoming King.

If the ambassadors thought that the baby looked healthy, then his father and mother could expect offers of suitable brides to start coming in for him even before he reached his first birthday. The marriages of royal children were arranged early: the little Archduchess Margaret of Austria, fifty years earlier, had been a divorcee by the age of 8, and the younger of the two Princes in the Tower had already been two years a widower when he disappeared into the Tower at the age of 10. But the marriage of this little English prince would be especially important, because the events leading up to his birth had rocked Europe, and because now his actual arrival would finally give England a male heir after twenty-four years without one.

The people of England knew by bitter experience how important it was to have a prince whom everyone recognized as the rightful heir to the throne. In the previous century, two rival families, Lancaster and York, had both claimed the crown, and the resulting quarrel had given rise to the Wars of the Roses, which had finally ended less than fifty years earlier, in 1485, when King Henry VII defeated and killed Richard III at the Battle of Bosworth and seized the throne. During the Wars of the Roses almost all the rival claimants to the throne had been killed, and when King Henry VII, as the last remaining representative of the House of Lancaster, married Elizabeth of York, peace was finally ensured. But it was a precarious peace, because although King Henry and Queen Elizabeth had seven children, only two daughters and one son, King Henry VIII, had reached adulthood; and although King Henry VIII had been on the throne for twenty-five years now, his only children were a daughter and an illegitimate son. He had been so worried about the question of the succession that he had even contemplated trying to get his illegitimate son recognized as his heir; but then, at 16, the boy had died, and all Henry VIII had left now was his daughter, Mary.

A daughter, however, was no use. Once, back in the twelfth century, a woman, Matilda, had tried to rule England as Queen in her own right; but even though her father, King Henry I, before his death, had made all his barons promise to accept her, they went back on their promise as soon as he was dead and allowed Matilda's cousin Stephen to become King instead. When Matilda tried to enforce her claim England was plunged into nineteen years of civil war and virtual anarchy. That was what had happened the last time the heiress to the throne had been a woman, and nobody was anxious to repeat the experiment.

So when Henry VIII realized that his first wife, Queen Catherine of Aragon, had grown too old to bear him any more children, he began to think about divorcing her. Since England was a Catholic country, he would need the consent of the Pope to do this; but when an heir to a kingdom was needed Popes had traditionally been willing to lend a sympathetic ear to requests for annulments of royal marriages. Also, Queen Catherine's first husband had been Henry VIII's elder brother, who had died when he was 15, and there was a passage in the Bible which forbade a man to marry his brother's wife, threatening him with childlessness if he did so. Henry and Catherine were not childless, but having only a daughter was just as bad, so Henry could use this passage to strengthen his case.

Normally, the Pope would probably have granted Henry's request fairly readily. Popes knew as well as anyone the importance of having an heir to a kingdom. But the Pope at the moment was not a free agent. For a long time now Italy had been the greatest centre of art and learning in Europe, but it had also been one of the most politically disorganized countries in Europe. It consisted of a lot of little duchies and cities with no overall ruler, and this provided a great temptation to the kings of France and Spain, who decided to invade Italy and seize it for themselves. The Spanish got there first, sending a fleet and taking over the kingdom of Naples, which then included all of the southern part of the country; then the French marched over the Alps and tried to conquer the northern duchy of Milan. During one of their periodic wars, the troops of the Spanish king captured Rome. The Pope thus became a prisoner of the Spanish—and the King of Spain was the nephew of Catherine of Aragon. The Pope could not possibly offend his powerful captor by agreeing to the divorce of his aunt.

By this time, though, Henry VIII had a personal as well as a political reason for wanting to be divorced from his wife. He had fallen in love with Anne Boleyn, the French-educated daughter of one of his courtiers. Although Henry had been in love before, this time it was different, because Anne, unlike her predecessors, refused to become Henry's mistress. She said it must be marriage or nothing; so Henry agreed to marry her and make her Queen. First, though, he had to divorce Queen Catherine. Henry spent six years trying to persuade the Pope to do this, but without success. Anne began to think she would never become Queen; but there was one last card she could play. After keeping Henry waiting for six years, she finally agreed to become his mistress—and became pregnant. Now Henry could not afford to wait any longer, for the baby had to be born in wedlock if he was to be sure of it succeeding peacefully to the throne.

One of Henry's ministers, a man named Thomas Cromwell, suggested to him a way out of all his difficulties. Henry should stop waiting for permission from the Pope, said Cromwell—indeed he should forget about the Pope altogether. Instead he should break away from the authority of the Catholic church and set up his own Church of England. This would achieve two highly desirable objects: the new church would give Henry his divorce immediately, so he could marry Anne; and Henry would also be able to claim for himself the vast wealth of the church, to which generations of Englishmen and women had been giving money and land in the hope of winning favour in the eyes of God. Most importantly of all, once Henry and Anne were married her child would be legitimate, and could therefore inherit the throne of England. All the disadvantages of the new church—the fact that it alienated England from powerful, Catholic France and Spain, the fact that some people, personal friends of Henry's among them, preferred to die rather than renounce their allegiance to the Pope—all this paled into insignificance beside the fact that Henry would, at last, have a legitimate son to inherit his throne.

It would, of course, be a terrible disappointment to him if, after all this, Queen Anne's child should be a girl. But Henry could feel sure it was a boy, because all the astrologers and doctors he could find to consult assured him that it was. So letters were prepared, ready to be sent to all parts of the kingdom to announce the joyful news of the birth of a prince. Just as a precautionary measure, though, a little space was left in each of the letters after the word 'prince', so that, if the worst should happen, an 's' could be inserted to give the word 'princes', the usual spelling of the word 'princess' at the time.

It was a wise precaution, for the worst did happen. Despite all that the astrologers and doctors had promised, when Queen Anne's baby was born, between three and four in the afternoon, it was not the longed-for son but another useless daughter.

She was called Elizabeth after Henry VIII's mother, Elizabeth of York, and his grandmother, Elizabeth Woodville, and after Anne Boleyn's mother too. There were few celebrations to mark her birth, even though her elder half-sister Mary was displaced from the succession and Elizabeth was declared Princess of Wales in her stead. Not for long, though. Henry managed to forgive Anne Boleyn for bearing a daughter, but he could not forgive the fact that both her next two pregnancies ended in miscarriage. It was not for this that he had divorced Catherine of Aragon—and Catherine at least had been a dutiful and patient woman, while Anne, feeling her position threatened by her failure to bear a son, was becoming increasingly temperamental, given to alarming outbursts of hysteria and rage in which she did not hesitate to abuse even the King. There had always been plenty of people at court who had been sorry to see Catherine and the old church go out and Anne and the new one come in; now they began to find the King increasingly inclined to listen to them.

What finally sealed the fate of Queen Anne was, ironically enough, the death of her predecessor Queen Catherine. Kept in confinement and separated from her beloved daughter after her divorce, Catherine of Aragon soon succumbed to strain, poverty, cold and illness. Henry appeared delighted at the news, and instead of going into mourning for his former wife wore yellow to celebrate her death. But soon it became apparent to everyone at court that after the death of Catherine, Anne's days were numbered. The Pope, and the kings of France and Spain, had always refused to recognize that Henry's divorce from Catherine was valid; this meant that in their eyes he was not legally married to Anne, and they would therefore consider Elizabeth (or any other child of Anne) as illegitimate, and would depose her if they could. Worse still, Henry knew that many of his own subjects, although he had forced them on pain of death to swear an oath declaring Anne's children his only legitimate heirs, secretly did not believe it. After his death it was only too likely that fighting would break out between supporters of Catherine of Aragon's daughter Mary and Anne Boleyn's daughter Elizabeth. He was no nearer having an undisputed heir than he had ever been.

As long as Catherine of Aragon lived many people would still think she was the rightful Queen. So it would be no good divorcing Anne Boleyn to marry yet a third Queen who might bear him a son: in the eyes of his people his next marriage would not be legal either. But once Catherine died everything changed. Now, if he got rid of Anne, everyone—even followers of the Pope—would recognize a third marriage as legal, whereas before they would have thought it bigamous.

It was an easy matter to trump up charges of adultery against Anne, and adultery, for a Queen, was high treason, and so punishable by death. Just for good measure other charges were also brought against her: she was accused of incest with her own brother, perhaps so that he too could be got rid of and the lands and titles with which Henry had showered him given to someone else, and she was also accused of witchcraft. She had a tiny sixth finger on her left hand which she was always careful to keep covered up in the folds of her dress; one of the only acts of malice ever recorded of Catherine of Aragon is that when Anne first caught Henry's eye, Catherine used to make Anne play cards with her in Henry's presence, because both hands are needed to play at cards and so Anne was unable to keep her deformity concealed. In an age when any physical deformity was readily accepted as being a mark of the devil, it was easy to accuse Anne of witchcraft, and perhaps saying that his wife was a witch made Henry feel less of a fool for having devoted six years of his life to trying to marry her and then changing his mind about it so quickly. He could simply say that she had cast a spell on him.

Whatever they might have thought about Anne's guilt or innocence, no one on the committee which tried her—which included her uncle and the man to whom she had been engaged before Henry snapped her up—would have dared to find her anything other than guilty when it was obvious that was the verdict the king wanted. The only mercy she was allowed was to have a sharp sword brought especially from Calais to cut off her head (the usual means of execution, the axe, could often take several blows to complete the job). So when Anne was led out to her execution, on 19 May 1536, she at least had the blessing of a swift death.

But Anne was not only executed; she was also divorced, and her marriage, like Catherine's before her, was declared null and void. This meant that Elizabeth, like her elder half-sister Mary, was illegitimate, and no longer eligible to succeed to the throne. The little girl was not yet 3, but she detected the transformation at once. 'How now?' she asked. 'Yesterday my lady Princess, today my lady Elizabeth? How comes it?' Her words revealed that, young as she was, she had already learned two important lessons: the insecurity of her own position, and the importance of the trappings of rank, of outward shows, signs, and symbols. She was never to forget either of those lessons.

Only ten days after the execution of Anne Boleyn, Henry VIII married for the third time. His new wife was Jane Seymour, who had been one of Queen Anne's Maids of Honour. Jane was quiet and rather plain, and seems at the time of her marriage to have been at least 25 years old, quite an advanced age for a first marriage in Tudor times. She came, though, from a family with a good record for producing boys, and she was very modest and meek—qualities which made her the exact opposite of Queen Anne, which may perhaps have been why Henry was attracted to her. Queen Jane was very religious, and she favoured the old, Catholic ways, which at first got her into trouble with Henry. Soon, though, they both had other things to think about, for Queen Jane discovered that she was pregnant.

Once again England made ready for the birth of an heir. Queen Jane went to Hampton Court to await the arrival of her baby, but Henry stayed away, as there was said to be plague in the area and he was reluctant to expose himself to the risk of catching it. He seems not to have worried so much about the risk to his wife and unborn child; perhaps he feared that the baby would be yet another daughter, and so not worth taking special precautions for. But when the child was born, on 12 October 1537, it was not a daughter, but the longed-for son.

His delighted father named the baby Edward, because the news of the birth had reached him on St. Edward's Day. The christening was held the next Sunday; christenings had to take place soon after the birth because so many babies died young, and a child who died unbaptized was thought to be unable to go to heaven. The courtiers were told to bring only a few people with them because the more people they were, the more likely it was that one of them might be carrying an infectious disease, and Henry had waited too long for a son to take any risks. The train of the baby prince's christening gown was carried by his two half-sisters—Catherine of Aragon's daughter Mary and Anne Boleyn's daughter Elizabeth. Although both girls had been declared illegitimate by their father, Queen Jane had persuaded him to behave affectionately towards them and let them come to court sometimes.

But Queen Jane herself took no part in the christening ceremonies. She had had a difficult labour—a popular song of the time went 'Queen Jane lay in labour/Nine days and more'—and in the end the baby may have been delivered by caesarean section. Queen Jane never recovered from the birth. At the little prince's christening she could only lie on a couch, propped up by pillows, and look on; and less than two weeks later she died. King Henry's chief minister, in an interesting display of the poor medical knowledge of the period, said she died because her attendants had foolishly allowed her to eat whatever she pleased, and to get too cold.

Although King Henry had divorced his first wife and beheaded his second, he was genuinely upset by the death of his third. He had Queen Jane buried at Windsor in the tomb he was preparing for himself—she was the only one of his wives to be allowed to share his grave—and, ten years later, it is said to have been her name that was on his lips when he died. Meanwhile, though, he soon began to look around for a new wife. His ministers persuaded him to choose Anne of Cleves, a Protestant princess whose family would be useful allies now that Henry, by breaking with Rome, had alienated the powerful kings of France and Spain, both orthodox Catholics. Unfortunately, Henry took a great dislike to Anne of Cleves, and two months after the marriage he divorced

14

her on the grounds of non-consummation. Anne was wise enough to put up no resistance—she did not want to share the fate of Anne Boleyn—and lived quietly in England with the honorary title of 'King's Sister', surviving her husband by more than ten years.

One of the reasons why Henry was so anxious to get rid of Anne of Cleves was that he had, once again, fallen in love. This time his choice was a young girl called Catherine Howard, who was English, a niece of the Duke of Norfolk, and, strangely, a cousin of Queen Anne Boleyn. Catherine, like Anne Boleyn and Jane Seymour, had caught the king's eye while serving as Maid of Honour to her predecessor, in this case Anne of Cleves. We know less about Catherine Howard than about any other of Henry's queens—there is no surviving portrait of her, and we do not even know how old she was when Henry married her; her enemies later put about a story that she had pretended to be younger than she really was by saying she was her father's youngest daughter (who had in fact died as a child) when she was really one of the older ones. We do know, however, that she had been brought up in the household of her step-grandmother, the Dowager Duchess of Norfolk, at Lambeth, and that she, like almost all the Howard family, still adhered to the old, Catholic ways. Indeed Catherine seems to have been deliberately introduced to the King by supporters of Catholicism, who had been alarmed at his previous marriage to the Protestant Anne of Cleves and wanted to influence his thinking in their own favour.

Once introduced, Catherine quickly charmed the King, and they were married sixteen days after his divorce from Anne of Cleves. Henry loaded his young wife with jewels and called her his 'rose without a thorn'. The court seemed full of sunshine again, and Henry, although he was now ageing rapidly, grossly overweight and suffering from a suppurating ulcer on his leg, seemed like a young man again. Because Catherine Howard was Anne Boleyn's first cousin, she was especially kind to the little Elizabeth, who was by this time a clever, serious, well-educated child of 7, already making good progress in Italian, French, Greek and Latin; by the age of 16 she was to speak all of them fluently.

Then, only eighteen months after her marriage, tragedy struck Queen Catherine Howard. She was young, beautiful, adored—but she was also foolish. She had not been brought up to be a queen, and no one had kept a particularly close watch on her in her step-grandmother's house at Lambeth. Catherine had slept in a large dormitory with the other girls of the house—and now it emerged that young men had been in the habit of visiting the dormitory at night. Catherine had apparently become engaged to one of these young men and they had slept together. Worse still, after her marriage Catherine had become bored with the fat king with the ulcerous leg, and she had taken a lover. When the King travelled around the country, she and her lady-in-waiting would go on a tour of each new residence to find the most convenient route for smuggling the young man into her room. It was a dangerous game, and Catherine was bound to get caught eventually. Also, the faction at court which had supported the King's break with Rome and his Reformation of the English church was worried about the influence that Catherine and her Catholic family had over Henry. When they got wind of what was going on in Catherine's bedchamber they were only too delighted to tell the King all about it; and Catherine, like her cousin Anne Boleyn before her, was beheaded on Tower Green on 1 February 1542.

Once again, Elizabeth had lost someone who had been close to her. Fortunately for her, though, she was equally lucky in her next stepmother, though Henry's sixth choice of wife could not have been more different from Catherine Howard. Catherine Parr was 31, already twice widowed, though childless, and a clever woman with a taste for reading and a deep interest in the new religion that had been founded in Germany, Protestantism. She was also in love with someone else—Queen Jane Seymour's brother, Sir Thomas Seymour. But when he discovered that the King was interested in Catherine Parr, Seymour discreetly went abroad and Catherine became the King's sixth wife.

In many ways Catherine was an admirable Queen. She was a good nurse to Henry, patiently dressing his sore leg for him, and she was very kind to her three stepchildren, taking a particular interest in their education and encouraging and rewarding their progress. But in one area she was not pleasing to Henry, and that was her religion. Although Henry had broken with Rome, he had never embraced Protestantism. Nor had he any intention of so doing. What he was attempting to maintain was a sort of Catholicism-without-the-Pope, in which he himself enjoyed all the respect and authority which had traditionally been given to the Pope.

The words 'Protestant' and 'Catholic' are in some ways misleading ones to use, because in the sixteenth century it was not the actual theological differences between the two religions that mattered so much as the practical consequences of those differences. Especially in the countryside and among the poorer people, it is probable that very few people understood the theological differences; but everyone could feel the practical consequences. One of the principal differences between the two religions was that Catholicism maintained that the bread and wine consumed during the Communion service were transformed, by a miracle, into the actual body and blood of Christ, whereas Protestants thought that the bread and wine remained bread and wine, and were merely a symbolic representation of the body and blood of Christ. This Catholic belief was known as the doctrine of the Real Presence. Catholics also believed that the Virgin Mary and the saints could intercede with God on behalf of people's souls even after they were dead; Catholics thought that people who were not actually damned or saints, and who had not died in a state of grace, went to a place midway between heaven and hell called Purgatory, and that praying for them after their death could shorten their time in Purgatory. Protestants did not believe in Purgatory and abolished the paying of reverence to saints, seeing it as idolatry.

Even more important, though, was the fact that Catholics believed that if they confessed their sins to a priest, and carried out the punishment or 'penance' that he set them, then they were washed clean of those particular sins. Protestants, however, did not practise confession. Instead a Protestant was required to keep a sharp watch on his own soul, to keep it free from guilt and to discipline it if it strayed—to be, in effect, his own priest, with responsibility for his own spiritual welfare. It was also this aspect of Protestantism that probably most worried King Henry VIII. For Protestantism challenged not only the authority of the Pope, but also the authority of the priest, and so if effectively threatened the whole chain of power and command on which society had been based since mediaeval times.

For most of the mediaeval period, the kings of England had been at odds with the popes over their respective areas of authority. Usually the popes won, because they had in reserve a more powerful weapon than any the kings could wield: the popes, as the successors of St. Peter, were believed to hold the keys to heaven, and they could declare people who incurred their displeasure to be excommunicated—unable to receive communion or absolution, and so unable to go to Heaven. This was a prospect that terrified mediaeval Christians, and when in the thirteenth century the English king, John, had annoyed the Pope, the Pope had declared the entire land of England to be under an interdict, a sort of mass excommunication. John had eventually been forced to submit to the papal authority. But although popes and kings might quarrel about who should have more authority, the one thing that neither of them ever questioned was that some people, by virtue of their rank and status, had an automatic right to exert authority over people. Protestantism, by making everyone responsible for their own soul in the eyes of God, did call this principle into question. Some sixty years after the death of Henry VIII, King James I of England was asked by the more extreme Protestants to abolish the office of bishop. His reply showed that he knew exactly what was at stake. 'No,' he said. 'No bishops, no king.'

This, then, was why King Henry did not like Protestantism; so, although he had broken with the Pope, in many ways the practices of the English church were still Catholic. When Queen Jane Seymour died, for instance, masses had been said for her soul—a specifically Catholic practice, for Protestants believed that once you were dead the fate of your soul was irrevocably decided, either for good or for evil, and it was no use praying for it. Apart from the break with the Pope, Henry's most distinctive breaks with the past were the dissolution of the monasteries and the abolition of paying reverence to relics; and these two moves were taken not from any dislike of Catholic institutions, but for primarily financial reasons. Both monasteries and the relics of saints had, throughout the mediaeval period, attracted a great deal of money. People had gone on pilgrimages, as in Chaucer's *Canterbury Tales*, to the shrines where the relics of saints were kept, to ask for cures from illness or to pray for the birth of a child, and it was usual to accompany the prayers with an offering to the saint, perhaps a gold cup or a candlestick; and if the patient did indeed get better, or a child was indeed born, then the grateful pilgrim might perhaps return with a thank-offering. A similar system can still be found in operation in countries like Greece, where the shrines of saints are hung with donations like wristwatches—perhaps all somebody had to give—or with tiny models of the area where the person feels pain, like little eyes or ears made out of silver or plaster. Henry VIII himself had ridden to the shrine at Walsingham to give thanks for the birth of his first son by Catherine of Aragon, though the boy had died soon after. Now, though, the shrines were torn down—and all the valuables that had been given to them were seized by the King.

The monasteries were dissolved for the same reason. Over the centuries many people, hoping to find favour with God, had left money and lands to the monasteries; now, by getting rid of the monasteries, Henry could seize those rich pickings. He could also distribute the lands and even the monastery buildings among his courtiers and nobles to win their support; it was, after all, less than a century since the nobility of England had been making and breaking kings on the battlefield. Great houses like Lacock Abbey in Wiltshire and Stoneleigh Abbey in Warwickshire testify to monastic properties given to noble families by King Henry VIII.

But if this was Henry VIII's idea of a Reformation of the church, it was not everyone's. There were people who wanted not just to break with the Pope, but actually to turn England into a completely Protestant country. Queen Catherine Parr seems to have been one of these. Indeed it serves as an interesting image of the way the two factions,

Catholic and Protestant, competed for the minds of the King and country that Henry's six wives were alternately Catholic and Protestant: Catherine of Aragon a Catholic, Anne Boleyn an encourager of Protestantism, Jane Seymour inclined to Catholicism, Anne of Cleves a Protestant princess, Catherine Howard a member of a Catholic family, and Catherine Parr an intellectual who read Protestant books. In the case of each of the first five Queens, with the possible exception of Jane Seymour, the representatives of the contrary faith had pressed for the removal of each Queen in turn; and Catherine Parr was no exception.

Various Catholic members of the court were very alarmed by Catherine Parr's inclination to Protestantism. They discovered that, in the privacy of her own room, she read books by Protestants—and they told the King. Henry at once gave them a warrant for her arrest, and told them to look for her in the garden the next day. But perhaps Henry found Catherine too good a nurse to lose, or perhaps he was simply tired of divorcing and beheading his wives. At all events, he stage-managed a clever little scene. He let Catherine find out that she was going to be arrested, and when he heard her sobbing at the news, he went to her room and asked her what was the matter. Catherine at once said that she had never meant to set her opinion up above the King's; but, she tactfully added, she had been going to ask for his advice about what to think. 'Is it even so, sweetheart?' said the King. 'Then we are friends again.' When the Catholic counsellors came the next day to arrest Catherine in the garden, they found the King with her, and received the dressing-down of their lives.

Although other Protestants, including Anne Askew, the last woman to be racked in England, continued to be tortured and executed, Catherine Parr was left in peace for the remainder of her time as Henry's Queen. But that time was not long. On 28 January 1547, King Henry VIII breathed his last.

He was succeeded by his only son, Edward, who at 10 years of age now became King Edward VI. One of Henry's last acts before he died was to settle the succession, with

Edward first, his two half-sisters Mary and Elizabeth, now declared legitimate again, second and third, and after them the children of Mary, Henry's younger and favourite sister. The children of his elder sister Margaret, Queen of Scots, were excluded on the ground that they were Scottish and therefore foreign; and also Henry, ironically enough, had fallen out with Margaret because she had been divorced. Because England, despite the break with the Pope, was still basically a Catholic country, a Requiem Mass was sung for the soul of Henry VIII; but the new King Edward, although his mother Jane Seymour had been inclined to Catholicism, was fervently in favour of Protestantism. This may have been due partly to his stepmother Catherine Parr, who had taken a great interest in his education, and partly to his own temperament, for he was a very thoughtful, introspective and immensely learned boy, and the Protestant emphasis on the need to be the monitor of your own soul made it attractive to intellectuals.

At 10, however, he was still far too young to govern. The real ruler of the land, called the 'Protector', was Edward's uncle, Jane Seymour's brother Edward, Duke of Somerset. King Edward had another uncle, too—the Duke of Somerset's younger brother Sir Thomas Seymour. He was a very handsome and lively man, with a great appetite for power, and he seems to have thought that one way of getting it would be to marry the widowed Queen Catherine Parr. He had already been on the point of proposing to her once before when Henry VIII had stepped in; now they agreed to marry. Seymour took Catherine to his Gloucestershire home, Sudeley Castle, and with them went the young Elizabeth, who was in Catherine's care. The Duke of Somerset was very alarmed by this marriage, for he thought that his brother was probably plotting in some way to gain power.

Somerset was right. Sir Thomas Seymour was indeed plotting mischief, although his ambition seems to have been much greater than his planning ability, and it is unclear quite what he was trying to achieve. Queen Catherine Parr was now pregnant. She was in her mid-thirties, a dangerously late age at which to have a first baby in Tudor times, and she herself had a strong premonition that she would not survive

21

the birth. Thomas Seymour could well expect to be a widower in a few months' time, and he had set his sights high for his next bride. He had started to flirt with the 14-year-old Princess Elizabeth. He took to entering her chamber dressed in little more than his shirt, and to teasing and romping with her. Queen Catherine Parr found them playing together in a way that might have seemed like innocent fun to a lively teenager but suggested darker things to an experienced woman, and the depression into which this plunged the widowed Queen made her pregnancy even more difficult. A week after the birth of her daughter, in August 1548, she died. It is presumed, though not certain, that the baby also died before reaching adulthood.

Thomas Seymour, however, never made the grand second marriage of which he dreamed. His own brother, the Duke of Somerset, had him arrested and executed. Once again, Elizabeth had lost someone close to her to the axe; but she had learned not to show her feelings. When told of Seymour's execution she merely replied, 'This day died a man of much wit and small judgement.'

The Duke of Somerset himself did not live long to triumph over his brother's death. His powerful enemy, the Duke of Northumberland, resented Somerset's monopoly of authority, and eventually managed to topple Somerset and persuade the King to sign his death warrant. Northumberland played on the fears of the Protestants in order to do this. Although King Edward was himself a Protestant, if he died the next heir would be his half-sister Mary, an earnest Catholic. She would undoubtedly try to reverse the Reformation, and the Protestants who had come to power under Edward VI would lose their jobs and perhaps their lives. Northumberland persuaded them that the only way to avoid this was to bypass the terms of Henry VIII's will and persuade King Edward to agree to an alternative heir. By the time the boy-king was 16, it was obvious that this was a matter of some urgency, for Edward was ill, suffering from the then-fatal disease of tuberculosis. He could not live long.

The Duke of Northumberland could have proposed Princess Elizabeth as the alternative heir, for she was Protestant. But he did not. Henry VIII had stipulated in his will that after Edward, Mary and Elizabeth, the succession should pass to the children of his younger sister Mary, the princess after whom the ship the Mary Rose had been named. Mary herself had died before Henry, but she had left two daughters. The elder of these two daughters was Frances, Duchess of Suffolk, and she and her husband were both Protestants and allies of Northumberland. So the Duke and Duchess of Suffolk and the Duke of Northumberland came to an agreement: the Suffolks' eldest daughter, Lady Jane Grey, should be declared heir to the crown, and at the same time she should marry the Duke of Northumberland's son, Lord Guildford Dudley. King Edward VI was persuaded to agree to all this just before he died.

But the people of England did not agree. Many of them were still in favour of Catholicism, and perhaps more importantly they knew that Henry VIII's daughter Mary was the rightful heir. They flocked to her standard, and after a reign of only nine days, Lady Jane and her husband were arrested and imprisoned in the Tower. Although Jane was only 16 and had never wanted to be Queen, Mary had her, her husband and the Duke of Northumberland beheaded.

Queen Mary, as the Protestants had feared, immediately restored full-scale Catholicism to England, and declared that the Pope was once again head of the English church. She chose for her husband her Catholic, Spanish cousin Philip, heir to the throne of Spain, whose grandmother had been Catherine of Aragon's sister. Mary looked forward eagerly to starting a new Catholic dynasty in England. But she was already 37, and in poor health from her years of disgrace and poverty, and her chances of conceiving seemed small. Nevertheless, she did after a while begin to display signs of pregnancy, and was overjoyed. But as the months wore on it became apparent that Mary was not pregnant at all; she was suffering either from the painful and eventually fatal disease of dropsy, which causes the body to swell, or from some sort of tumour. Her husband, despairing of having a son who would unite England and Spain, left the country, and poor Mary was left alone with her grief.

Not only had she failed to produce a child, she faced the almost unbearable prospect of having to leave England, when she died, to a Protestant successor—her half-sister Elizabeth. Mary had done what she could to restore Catholicism, and in an eager but ill-judged attempt to root out Protestantism she had burned alive many people who would not renounce it; she had even imprisoned Elizabeth in the Tower of London, but had been unable to find any evidence that she was plotting with Protestants so had been forced to release her again. Now, as Mary at the age of 43 lay dying of dropsy during the autumn of 1558, she knew that Elizabeth would succeed her and that her work for Catholicism would be fruitless. With her mind still on the baby she had wanted so badly, she died with her prayer book open at the page for the churching of women—the ceremony performed the first time a woman goes to church after the birth of a baby. The Catholic Queen was dead, and the Elizabethan era had begun.

II

The Virgin Queen

ELIZABETH was 25 years old when, on 17 November 1558, she became Queen of England. The story goes that the messengers found her sitting under an oak tree reading the Bible in Greek in the grounds of the old palace of Hatfield, where she had spent much of her childhood and where she had been living quietly during the last dangerous years of Mary's reign. When they told her that her sister was dead and she was now Queen she knelt on the grass and said in Latin 'It is the Lord's doing and marvellous in our eyes.' She had waited for this for five long years; now at last she was free from the danger that had hung over her throughout her sister's reign.

Her problems, however, were not over yet, and she knew it. The England that she had inherited was terrifyingly isolated against the mighty Catholic powers of France and Spain. Fortunately, the kings of Spain and France hated each other only slightly less than they hated Protestantism, and for the time being at least there was little prospect of them entering into an alliance against England; but at any moment a dynastic marriage or a new treaty might change the situation, and unite them against her. Even more pressing, however, was the fact that England itself was a country racked by internal religious dissension. In some parts of the country, particularly in London, the counties around it, and the university towns of Oxford and Cambridge, the new religion of Protestantism had begun to attract a following; some people, indeed, had felt so strongly about the new faith that during the persecution of Protestants in the reign of Queen Mary they had chosen to be burned alive rather than renounce their religion. In other parts of the country, however, and especially in the remoter areas like Devon,

25

Cornwall, Lancashire and the north country, Catholicism was still very strong indeed. For Elizabeth to declare herself decisively in favour of either of the two faiths was to risk alienating an important part of her country.

Fortunately, it went against every instinct Elizabeth had to do anything decisive at all. All her life her preference was to play for time, to compromise, to resist at all costs any burning of her bridges or narrowing of her options; and although it frequently drove her ministers to distraction, it was a policy that always served her well. Although Elizabeth, like her brother Edward, was herself a Protestant, having been brought up under Protestant tutors, she had no desire to persecute people for not having the same religious beliefs as she did, provided they gave her no trouble and conformed outwardly to her state religion; she said in a famous phrase, 'I do not wish to make windows into men's souls.' So the religious policy which her government eventually adopted, known as the Elizabethan settlement, was meant to act as a sort of half-way house between Protestantism and Catholicism, something with which everybody could feel comfortable.

Elizabeth herself would ideally have liked a return to the neither-one-thing-nor-the-other religion of her father King Henry VIII, a sort of modified Catholicism without the Pope. But when her first Parliament met, in January 1559, it became apparent that most of the members of the House of Commons would not be satisfied with the prayer book that had been used in Henry VIII's reign; they insisted that the Protestant prayer book which had been introduced by King Edward VI should be used instead. Elizabeth agreed, but deleted from it some of the more extreme Protestant practices and some insulting references to Catholicism. When her religious settlement was eventually put into practice, a traveller from France was amazed to see the Protestant Queen of England behaving at church for all the world as if she were a Catholic.

Like all compromises, however, Elizabeth's religious settlement failed to please the more extreme members of the two faiths. The situation also grew much worse when in 1570, twelve years after the start of her reign, Pope Pius V published a declaration saying that since Elizabeth was a heretic, her Catholic subjects no longer owed allegiance to her. This effectively opened the way for Elizabeth to be assassinated by an English Catholic. Now that her own life and throne were thus placed in danger, Elizabeth began to adopt a much sterner attitude towards Catholics, culminating in 1587 in the execution of her cousin Mary, Queen of Scots, who had a strong claim to the throne and who had therefore become the focus of Catholic plots to assassinate Elizabeth. The death of Mary was a severe blow to the Catholic cause in England until the King of Spain, Philip II, who had once been married to Elizabeth's half-sister Queen Mary Tudor, declared that in her will Mary, Queen of Scots, had assigned to him all her rights to the throne of England and that he was therefore going to invade to claim them. In 1588, the year after the death of Mary, Queen of Scots, he launched his great armada, a fleet of ships, against England—but barely had it arrived in the English Channel when it was scattered by a great storm which English Protestants saw as a 'Protestant wind' sent by God to help them.

The defeat of the Armada gave a great boost to English Protestantism and English national pride. At last it seemed possible that what Elizabeth had been hoping for from the beginning of her reign might begin to happen: the followers of the 'Old Religion', as Catholicism was sometimes called, might just begin to die out naturally. With no new priests being ordained, and as the last of the generation which had been brought up in the old faith died away, Protestantism could take root painlessly and naturally. Catholicism had plenty of fight left in it yet, though. In order that this should not happen, young Englishmen took to stealing across to the Continent and being trained as priests at Catholic seminaries there, and then re-entering England in secret to live and to celebrate the Mass in secret meeting-places. It was this practice that led to the construction of priests' holes, concealed rooms or passages which are still to be seen in some Elizabethan country houses, so that if the authorities came searching, the priest could be hidden until they had gone. If he was captured, he faced certain death.

But although Elizabeth executed priests, she did not deal so harshly with ordinary Catholics; indeed, in all the forty-five years of her reign she killed exactly the same number of Catholics as her sister Mary had burned Protestants in only five years on the throne. Instead she tried to deter them from the practice of their faith by introducing stiff fines for those who did not attend Protestant services every Sunday. Some people went to the Protestant church but remained secret Catholics; others preferred to pay the fines or even risk being put in prison. Nothing Elizabeth did seemed to make any difference: Catholicism was indestructible.

There were many reasons why the Old Religion died so hard. One of these was that it was, in the sixteenth century, in many ways a more comforting religion than Protestantism: a Protestant had to live with the constant self-examination of his own soul, keeping it from sin and bearing the weight of guilt if he did lapse, whereas a Catholic could confess to his priest, perform a penance, receive absolution, and be once again pure and guiltless in the sight of God. Catholics, too, could pray to the saints and the Virgin Mary to intercede with God on their behalf; and there was a whole host of comforting folktales which told how the Virgin in particular was always ready to lend a willing ear to petty criminals and minor sinners if they asked her nicely enough. Catholics could even know that once they were dead they could still profit from the prayers said on their behalf by their friends and relatives and by the church. To become a Protestant was to forego all this security.

There were other aspects of Catholicism which were deeply attractive to many people. For one thing, Protestant church services tended to be much simpler than Catholic ones; since Protestants placed the emphasis on the interaction of the individual soul with God, they were not so much interested in the ritual and the outward observation and ceremonies which were such an important part of Catholicism. They saw these things as a poor substitute for genuine, heartfelt devotion; it was this attitude, taken to extremes, which in the next century led extreme Protestants to legislate against the celebration of Christmas and to forbid dancing, music-making and playgoing as works of the Devil. Many

28

people, however, derived a deep psychological fulfilment from marking the important days of the year with rites and special observances, and in particular there was considerable popular attachment to the Catholic practice of dividing the year up into a cycle of fast days and feasting days. This gave a shape and pattern to people's existence and provided a counterpoint to the routine of their everyday lives, and they were very reluctant to abandon it. As a matter of fact the English Catholics were even prepared to go against the Pope in this. As the sixteenth century wore on, the Pope and his advisers had become increasingly concerned about the impact of Protestantism, and had attempted to reform some of the practices of the church which had been most vehemently attacked. In particular, they had tried to make Catholicism seem a more spiritual and less worldly religion, and the Pope let it be known that he felt it might be wise to stop laying so much emphasis on the feasting and fasting cycle. English Catholics, however, would have none of this. They continued to observe the cycle, and it even became the practice for families to invite their neighbours to share the times of feast with them, which of course served to strengthen the bonds within the Catholic community.

This was not the only point on which English Catholics were prepared to disobey the Pope. Although he had declared it legitimate for them to rebel against Elizabeth and even to assassinate her, only a tiny percentage of them made any attempt to do either; and when Philip of Spain sent the great Catholic Armada against England, Elizabeth received many offers from Catholics anxious to fight for her against the Spanish. The English Catholics might be Catholic, but they were also, and in most cases primarily, English, and quite willing to share in the traditional distrust of the Pope and of all other foreigners that had largely characterized Catholicism in England since early mediaeval times. It was not love of the Pope that kept them faithful to the Old Religion, but the sense that it filled a gap in their lives that Protestantism would leave empty.

One notable aspect of English Catholicism at this period is that it seems to have been women, in particular, who clung to the old faith. It was women who superintended the catering at the times of feast and fast, women, in many cases, who made the economies needed to pay the fines for non-attendance at church, women who supervised their household and kept it together when their husbands were in prison for their religion; and there are many stories from the period of wives encouraging husbands, and mothers sons, to stay true to the faith. The explanation for this may well be that women had most to lose by abandoning Catholicism. It is sometimes said that Catholicism is a religion that is hostile to women, but this was not how it was perceived in the sixteenth century; if anything, it was Protestantism that was seen as undervaluing women and denying them any meaningful rôle to play. In the more extreme Protestant circles it was even suggested that the wife, now that she no longer confessed to the priest, should confess to her husband instead, and that he should take charge of her spiritual welfare; the lack of emphasis on feasting deprived women of the one form of control they had traditionally enjoyed; and Protestantism also not only abolished the reverence of female saints along with the male, but virtually ignored the Virgin Mary, so central a figure in Catholicism: indeed some Protestants went so far as to refer to her simply as 'Moll, God's maid'. Thus women were robbed not only of the prayers of the interceding saints and Virgin, but also of any positive female rôle models.

At the same time, the dissolution of the monasteries had included that of convents, which had traditionally been the only sources of education for girls and had also represented the only alternative to marriage and children, allowing, at least to the women who could rise to office in them, something faintly resembling a career. Now all that was gone, and it seems that women felt its loss. Although the wealthier Catholics could and did still send their daughters to convents abroad to be educated or to take the veil, this was impossible for poorer people; and when, in the early part of the seventeenth century, some bold women attempted to set up a sort of seminary for women, they were told that in the eyes of the law there was no such thing as a single woman. The law classified all women as either 'married' or 'going to be married', and an Elizabethan proverb declared that old maids, having no children to lead them into heaven, would instead pay for their defiance of the natural order of things by leading apes in hell—as when Katherina, in Shakespeare's *The Taming of the Shrew*, tells her father Baptista that he loves her sister Bianca better than her:

> I must dance barefoot on her wedding-day,
> And for your love to her lead apes in hell.

> (II, i, 33–4)

It is impossible to know how much Elizabeth understood of the motives which actuated her Catholic subjects, but it does look as though she was, either consciously or subconsciously, aware of some of the gaps that had been left in people's lives by the introduction of Protestantism. About some of them, such as the lack of confession and the demotion of the saints, there was nothing to be done; they were simply inalienable parts of Protestantism. There might be ways, though, of compensation in part for the loss of ritual, of the fasting and feasting cycle, and of positive female rôle models. Although the new church services were simple, there were other areas of life into which ritual could be introduced; new feasts and holidays could be declared in honour of other occasions. And a new, splendid, Virgin could be found—the Queen herself.

So began the cult of Queen Elizabeth, which, whether it was deliberately planned or naturally evolved or a mixture of both, became the distinguishing feature of life at the Elizabethan court. At the outset of her reign, however, there was no hint of it; indeed it would have seemed unthinkable, because it was taken absolutely for granted that the Queen would marry. It was just as essential for her to have an heir as it had been for her father, and anyway all women married. The only question was whom she should marry. There was no shortage of candidates, but since Elizabeth's husband, as her half-sister Mary Tudor's had been, would be given the title of King and would quite probably become the effective ruler of England, while Elizabeth settled down to having children, it was of the utmost importance to make the best possible choice.

The field of choice was wide. Since France and Spain each

distrusted the other, each was very anxious to secure an alliance with England, especially if this meant that Elizabeth would convert to Catholicism. So almost as soon as Elizabeth succeeded to the throne a messenger came from King Philip of Spain, widower of her half-sister Queen Mary Tudor, proposing to her; there was also another member of his family, the Archduke Charles of Austria, who was suggested at various times, not to mention the French princes, the Dukes of Alençon and Anjou, and King Eric of Sweden. King Eric pursued her with particular ardour: in the early years of her reign he sent her eighteen large piebald horses and two shiploads of treasure, and announced his intention of visiting her, until Elizabeth dissuaded him. Even then he still sent his sister, who landed in England only two days before the birth of her baby, to which Elizabeth was godmother. Eventually, however, poor King Eric despaired of winning Elizabeth's hand and outraged his people by marrying the daughter of a common soldier; he later went mad and had to be confined to a cell.

To all her suitors, however, Elizabeth returned polite but non-committal answers. The reason for this could have been policy. As long as both France and Spain thought they might win her over, they would continue to be friendly to her, and the danger of an attack from either of them would vanish; but as soon as she committed herself to one, the other would become her enemy. The disadvantages of that, however, should have been outweighed by the fact that she would have a sure ally in whichever of the two she had chosen, so that although this might be a good reason for deferring her marriage for a short time while she sorted out the religious question, it was no reason for not making a decision eventually. Yet Elizabeth showed no sign of making a decision, and resisted all attempts to put pressure on her to do so. And as time dragged by her subjects began to suspect that there might be something else to account for her reluctance to accept a prince from either France or Spain.

From the beginning of her reign there had been a small number of people who felt that Elizabeth ought not to marry a foreigner at all, but one of her own subjects. They had seen what had happened to England when Philip of Spain had briefly been its King, and how easily he had been able to persuade Queen Mary to put his interests first in everything. Indeed, the English feeling that Spain was the national enemy dated almost entirely from Philip's brief stay there; before that Spain and England had traditionally been allies against France. It was suggested that Elizabeth could perhaps marry her cousin, Lord Hunsdon, whose Protestant credentials were impeccable and who had some claim to the throne in his own right. An Englishman, it was said, was the best person to govern England and to look after her interests. But it soon began to be observed that if Elizabeth did favour a subject, it was not Lord Hunsdon who was the man.

Even before she became Queen, she had met a young man called Robert Dudley. Dudley was the son of the same Duke of Northumberland who in the reign of Edward VI had tried to engineer the succession of Lady Jane Grey, and had married her to his son, Guildford Dudley, the younger brother of Robert. When the rebellion failed and Mary came to the throne Lady Jane, her husband Guildford, and the Duke of Northumberland had all been executed, and the Duke's four other sons, Robert among them, had been imprisoned in the Tower of London—the carvings they did there can still be seen on the wall of a cell in the Beauchamp Tower. A little while later the young Princess Elizabeth, suspected of conspiring with Protestants, was also sent to the Tower; and there she seems to have met Robert Dudley. The story runs that after they were both released he sold land to raise money for her, and that she never forgot it; whether that is true or not, it is certain that from the moment of Elizabeth's accession Dudley began a meteoric rise to power and fortune. First he was made Master of the Horse, an important post which meant he would always be near Elizabeth, and then he was created Earl of Leicester and given the large and impressive fortress of Kenilworth Castle in Warwickshire, while his brother Ambrose was given nearby Warwick Castle and made Earl of Warwick.

Rumours began to circulate that the Queen was in love with Leicester; at an official ceremony she was observed to tickle his neck, and some people did not hesitate to say that there was even more between them than that. It was commonly thought that the Queen would have liked to marry Leicester—if only he had not been married already.

Leicester's wife Amy Robsart, however, was kept well out of sight in the country. She was even rumoured to be ill. And then one day, having sent all the servants out for the day, she was found dead at the foot of a staircase, with her neck broken. Popular opinion immediately assumed that Leicester had murdered her to enable him to marry the Queen; some people even suggested that the Queen herself might have known about it. In recent years, medical research has suggested that Amy Robsart was in fact suffering from breast cancer, and that the cause of her death was a spontaneous fracture of the spine such as is sometimes suffered by women with advanced breast cancer. There is no longer any reason to suppose that Leicester, much less Elizabeth, had anything to do with her death. But medical knowledge in the sixteenth century had no way of making such a diagnosis, and Elizabeth must have known that for her to marry Leicester now that he was suspected of his wife's murder would be madness. How wise she was not to do so is shown by the furore which erupted in Scotland, not many years later, when her cousin Mary, Queen of Scots, married as her third husband the man who was suspected of her second husband's murder—and lost her throne as a result.

Just because she could not marry Leicester, however, did not mean that she would necessarily marry anybody else. Although she seemed delighted to receive proposals, and to be told by the ambassadors of foreign princes that she was the most beautiful woman in the world and that their masters were half-mad with love of her, the years went by and she still showed no sign of being about to make a decision. Parliament became increasingly anxious, especially after Elizabeth caught smallpox and had a narrow escape from death. The members of the House of Commons appealed to her to marry, but Elizabeth rebutted them and told them that it was none of their business. Two playwrights even wrote a tragedy, *Gorboduc*, showing the disasters that could overtake a country where a ruler died without an undisputed heir; but all to no avail. Still Elizabeth did not marry. And gradually it occurred to her ministers and people that perhaps she might never marry.

It is not clear at what stage this idea occurred to Elizabeth herself. Some modern historians argue that Elizabeth had a deep psychological fear of marriage, caused by the traumatic events of her childhood. In later life, Elizabeth never spoke of her mother, Anne Boleyn; she had been only 3 at the time of her death, and perhaps she did not even remember her. She did, however, like to hear her mother kindly spoken of, and she promoted to the Archbishopric of Canterbury her mother's chaplain, Matthew Parker. Anne Boleyn, in her last days, had asked Parker to take special care of the little Elizabeth, and Parker, one of the few people who had spoken in favour of Anne after she fell victim to Henry VIII's anger, had said that after her death she had become 'A Queen in heaven'. Elizabeth also adopted the white falcon badge which her mother had used as a mark of identification for her followers and servants, and she always tried to keep on good terms with her Howard and Carey relations on her mother's side. It is certainly possible, then, that Elizabeth felt herself torn between loyalty to the memory of her mother, and loyalty to the memory of the father who had transmitted to her the crown of England but who had also executed her mother. As if this were not enough to give her ambivalent ideas about marriage, she had also seen two of her stepmothers, first Jane Seymour and then Catherine Parr (to whom she was very close) die as a result of childbirth, which would have brought home very vividly to her the possibility that if she were to marry to try to have a child who would be an heir for England, it was perfectly possible that she would die herself, that the child might die too, and that England could then be plunged into turmoil anyway. Indeed, if Elizabeth and her child were to die, then England would probably be even worse off than if Elizabeth died unmarried, because her widower, who would probably be a foreign prince, might well try to annex England, or at least to interfere in the country's domestic politics.

None of these were very encouraging reasons to marry. Elizabeth might well have been influenced, too, by the high number of unhappy marriages she had witnessed:

after the death of Jane Seymour her father had married Anne of Cleves, and had divorced her after six months to marry Catherine Howard; and Catherine Howard herself had soon been beheaded for adultery. Catherine Howard had been a first cousin of Anne Boleyn, and had therefore been particularly kind to the little Elizabeth, who cannot have been unaffected by her death. Of Elizabeth's two aunts on her father's side, the elder, Margaret, Queen of Scotland, had divorced her second husband for adultery, and the younger, Mary, Duchess of Suffolk, had first been married off, against her will, to the King of France, and had then married for love, but had been loaded with crippling financial penalties for doing so by Henry VIII, and had also quarrelled with her second husband when they took different sides on the question of Henry VIII's divorce from Catherine of Aragon. After her father's death Elizabeth had gone to live with her stepmother Queen Catherine Parr and Catherine Parr's new husband Thomas Seymour; Seymour had rapidly begun to neglect Queen Catherine, who had become very depressed, in favour of pursuing Elizabeth herself, with a view to marrying her, and he had lost his head for it—yet another lesson to the young Elizabeth that marriage was a dangerous business. Next, she had seen her cousin Lady Jane Grey forced into a marriage she did not want with Lord Guildford Dudley, and manoeuvred by her new in-laws into a bid for the crown which cost Jane, too, her head; and lastly, Elizabeth had seen her own half-sister, Queen Mary I, have her heart half-broken by her phantom pregnancies and by the fact that her husband, Philip of Spain, whom she loved deeply, spent as little time as possible with her and, when he realized that she was unlikely ever to become pregnant, left the country altogether.

Elizabeth could also take warning from what happened to her cousin, Mary, Queen of Scots: Mary had fallen passionately in love with the good-looking Henry, Lord Darnley, married him, and given him the title of King—and discovered too late that he was a weak, easily-led, spoilt nincompoop, who may also have been infected with syphilis. After Darnley and his friends had broken into Mary's apartments when she was heavily pregnant and had stabbed to death, in front of her, an Italian musician whom they claimed (almost certainly wrongly) was her lover, Darnley was himself murdered—some said with Mary's connivance. Mary's position was now desperate, and it became even worse when she married the Earl of Bothwell, the man popularly believed to have murdered Darnley. Mary had little choice in the matter—it seems probable that Bothwell had abducted and raped her, and that, believing herself pregnant by him, she felt she must marry him—but her people would not tolerate what they regarded as her shameful behaviour: they rose up against her and imprisoned her. Bothwell was forced to flee abroad, and eventually died insane in a Danish dungeon, and when Mary did eventually escape she made the grave mistake of going to England, where Elizabeth, feeling that the presence of a Catholic heir to the throne was too grave a danger, imprisoned her once more and eventually executed her.

Having seen what disaster a rash marriage had brought upon Mary, Queen of Scots, and given such a family background, it would not be surprising if Elizabeth felt a reluctance to marry. Also, if she had a husband she would have to surrender to him all the power which she so much enjoyed exercising; instead of being Queen in her own right, she would become a secondary figure, important only as a potential producer of children. If she did not manage to have children, she would be regarded as a total failure, as her sister Queen Mary I had been; and it was perfectly possible that Elizabeth might not have children, for the record of her family was not encouraging. She herself was the only one of numerous children born to her father to reach healthy maturity (her sister Mary did live to be 37, but suffered from very poor health, and was of course unable to conceive); her mother Anne Boleyn had suffered several miscarriages after the birth of Elizabeth; her father's eldest sister, Margaret, Queen of Scotland, had had very difficult pregnancies, had lost babies during pregnancy and in infancy, and had produced only one son (who had himself died young) and one daughter; and her father's younger sister, Mary, Duchess of Suffolk, had lost a son in childhood and had produced two daughters who, along with their descendants, may have suffered from some form of restricted growth syndrome: the Duchess of Suffolk's granddaughter Lady Mary Grey was only four feet tall and a hunchback, and as well as that, both she and her sister died young. Elizabeth therefore had no reason to feel particularly optimistic about her ability to produce healthy children.

Lastly, although it was very rare indeed for royal ladies to remain unmarried, it was not quite without precedent. Margaret of Austria, who found herself at the age of 24 divorced once and widowed twice, had refused to marry again, preferring to act as Regent of the Netherlands, and Elizabeth's own stepmother, Anne of Cleves, had made no opposition whatever to being divorced by Henry; more, when her brother, the Duke of Cleves, had sent for her to come home, where there was the chance that she could be used in another diplomatic marriage, Anne had simply refused to go. Instead she had declared herself content to accept the title Henry VIII offered her of 'King's Sister', had accepted from him a present of a number of manor houses in the country, and had, apparently, lived a perfectly contented, single life until, having outlived both Henry and all his other wives, she died in 1557. Anne of Cleves must have been one of the few royal women known to Elizabeth whose situation could inspire envy instead of pity.

Elizabeth herself, however, although she sometimes declared that she intended to remain single, was always willing to listen to marriage proposals, and throughout her life she displayed a curiously ambivalent attitude towards marriage. Although she was herself responsible for her single state, with her characteristic indecisiveness she often showed signs of second thoughts or of regrets. When her cousin Mary, Queen of Scots, gave birth to a son Elizabeth exclaimed 'The Queen of Scots is lighter of a fair son, and I am but a barren stock'; and throughout her life, but especially in her later years, she was likely to react very badly to the love affairs and marriage plans of her Maids of Honour, particularly where these involved handsome young courtiers. She hated anything that reminded her of her own single state; and she preferred that the young men at her court should at least keep up the pretence of being interested only in her, for one of her foibles was that even in her very old age she still behaved, and liked to be treated, as though she were still young and desirable. Indeed she continued to discuss possible husbands long after she had passed the age of childbearing and when marriage would therefore have served no purpose. She was proposed to by her young cousin and heir-presumptive King James VI of Scotland, who even if he did not expect to be accepted was anxious to flatter her by making the suggestion; she kept the Austrian Archduke Charles waiting eight years for an answer; and as late as 1579, when she was 46, she still allowed the 23-year-old Duke of Alençon to come to England to court her: indeed she went so far as to write to Alençon's mother, Queen Catherine de' Medici, asking if it was true that Alençon had been marked by smallpox, as she did not want a disfigured husband. Queen Catherine encouragingly replied that a recent attack of measles had disguised the effects of the smallpox.

Indeed the Alençon marriage, ludicrous though it at first appeared, seemed on the verge of coming to completion. Queen Catherine had been promised by the astrologer Nostradamus that all her numerous children would be crowned kings or queens, and she was very anxious to see this come true; and since Alençon himself seems to have had no objection to becoming King Consort of England, he decided to speed up the usual slow rate of Elizabeth's decision-making processes by paying a surprise visit to England. Even though the Duke was very short and the smallpox marks were in fact still visible, Elizabeth seemed very taken with this ardent suitor, and allowed him to return on a formal visit to her, and at a tournament in Whitehall she even went so far as to take a ring from her finger and present it to him in public. Alençon, and many other people, seem to have regarded this as tantamount to agreeing to an engagement; but when it dawned on Elizabeth what she had done, her habitual horror of committing herself and a realization of what this step could mean overcame her liking for Alençon's wit and flattery. Her Maids of Honour, who were reluctant to see such a change, wept and wailed and prophesied doom: the people would cease to love her, she should remember how unhappy her sister Mary had been made by Philip of Spain, she should not waste herself on a mere youth, she should remember all the things she had so often said in praise of virginity. The next morning Elizabeth told Alençon she would never marry, but would instead think of him as a brother.

The hostile reaction of the Maids of Honour to the proposed marriage with Alençon, which had helped make up Elizabeth's mind to refuse him, was typical of the feeling in the court and in the country as a whole about the marriage. Sir Philip Sidney was banished from court for writing against it, and the Puritan John Stubbes was even more harshly treated for the same offence: both he and his publisher were sentenced to lose their right hands. Stubbes made a great impression on the crowd by raising his hat with his left hand as the blow fell and crying 'God save the Queen'; the incident did nothing to increase the popularity of Alençon, who throughout his visit was kept well away from the London populace in case of trouble. This reaction to the Alençon visit gives some indication of the difficulties Elizabeth would have had to contend with if she ever had decided to marry.

Alençon, however, represented Elizabeth's last serious prospect of matrimony. Although her doctors at the time of the Duke of Alençon's visit pronounced that she was still young enough and fit enough to have children, and although until a few months before her death at the age of 69 she was still able to dance a galliard every morning before breakfast, Elizabeth was obviously ageing, and equally obviously unwilling to face the fact. She was even losing her looks as her hair thinned, necessitating the wearing of wigs, and her teeth rotted away to blackened stumps. (The teeth of the English were notoriously prone to decay during this period, a fact ascribed by foreign observers to their inordinate fondness for sugar, which was frequently used in savoury dishes such as meat pies as well as in sweet ones.) Elizabeth had suffered toothache since earliest childhood, but it was not until 1578, when she was 45, that she was finally persuaded to have a tooth extracted, after the Bishop of London had offered to act as a guinea-pig by having one of his own pulled out first. Elizabeth's suffering was so much lessened by the extraction that she had several more pulled out, and it was reported that this made her very difficult to understand when she spoke quickly. Matters were made worse by her over-vigorous use of the gold and enamelled toothpicks which her Maids of Honour would give her as presents. These displaced her few remaining teeth and left them uneven. Elizabeth took considerable care over her appearance: she washed her hair with a compound made of wood-ash and water and whitened her skin with a concoction of egg white, poppy seeds and powdered egg-shell; she rubbed her teeth, while she still had them, inside and outside with a toothcloth; but nevertheless by the end of her reign she was driven to painting her face, her neck and her bosom in search of a youthful appearance, and to padding out her sunken cheeks by stuffing cloths inside them.

Elizabeth could not be unaware of the loss of her looks. For the last twenty years of her life no mirrors were allowed near her; if ever she went to the appartments of the Maids of Honour, all looking-glasses were hastily concealed. It was not until her last few weeks that she caused consternation amongst the court by again calling for a looking-glass, and when it came she complained bitterly about the flatterers who had told her that she was still as beautiful as ever. Even queens grow old; indeed Elizabeth could be said to have lasted remarkably well given that she had spent forty-five years grappling with a complex, interrelated series of problems, most of which, by their very nature, were liable to become more and more serious as her reign went on. The replacement of Catholicism by Protestantism had left a large gap in the lives of many of her subjects; her unmarried state worried the country and her advisers, and in some ways her as well, leaving her with a craving for affection, admiration and reassurance; and the combination of unrest at home and potential enemies abroad made her very anxious to create for herself an image of power and authority which might help bolster up the real weaknesses of her position. It was one of the great achievements of Elizabeth's reign that most of the

41

gravest of these problems were in fact solved, and solved by the same expedient.

The rulers of the Renaissance period had become particularly conscious of the importance of presenting a powerful and splendid appearance to their subjects and to their fellow-rulers. The trend had started in Italy and had gradually spread northwards across Europe, until one of the most important elements of the language of politics was a display of magnificence. There were several advantages in this for rulers: in the first place, however magnificent the pomp of the court, it was almost bound to cost less to maintain than more tangible symbols of power such as armies and fleets; and it also considerably augmented not only the prestige of the country but also the personal prestige of the ruler. The first of these reasons made it a particularly attractive option to Elizabeth, who had inherited from her grandfather King Henry VII an extremely careful attitude to money. And so gradually, as her reign progressed, more and more emphasis came to be placed on creating and elaborating an image for Elizabeth which would solve many of her most pressing problems: the image of the Virgin Queen.

It was a brilliantly original and daring conception. An unmarried Queen might be a liability, but the words 'Virgin Queen' had quite different connotations. They reminded people of the two Greek goddesses of mythology, Athene and Artemis, who had deliberately chosen to remain virgins and who, being goddesses, had remained eternally young and eternally beautiful, and this was a comparison which was bound to be particularly pleasing to Elizabeth, since not only could it help to divert her attention from the painful fact that in real life she *was* growing old and *was* losing her looks, but it also reflected onto her something of the aura of power and mystery which had surrounded the goddesses in classical legend. Furthermore, it was a sign of status in the Renaissance period to be familiar with classical literature and learning, and so associating Elizabeth with figures from classical mythology enhanced her status in this way too.

The image of the Virgin Queen had other advantages, too. It capitalized on Elizabeth's unmarried state instead of allowing it to be perceived as a weakness, and it also provided a very useful framework within which Elizabeth could conduct her relations with the handsome young men she liked to have about her at court. Early in her reign, when she was still relatively inexperienced, she had created scandal by her flirtation with Leicester; but a Virgin Queen could flirt as much as she liked—and Elizabeth did like, since it flattered her vanity and helped stave off her sense that she was getting old. She was able to use the image in much the same way as the code of courtly love had been used in earlier periods, as a safety-valve for emotions which it would otherwise have been difficult to express but painful to keep hidden. Handsome young courtiers could avow undying devotion to her, in hope of getting promotion at court, and she could gratefully accept their homage; everybody could thus be happy, and the whole thing could be safely governed by clearly defined rules.

But another use could also be made of the image of the Virgin Queen. As well as reminding people of the virgin goddesses of Greek mythology, it could also remind them of another, more important virgin: the Virgin Mary. If a gap had been left in people's lives by the disappearance of this powerful female rôle model, then perhaps it could be filled by the figure of a powerful female Queen. Elizabeth was always very careful not to press this too far; her successor, King James I, outraged public opinion by defending his relationship with George Villiers, Duke of Buckingham (almost certainly a homosexual one), with the words 'Christ had his John, and I have my George', but Elizabeth was never guilty of anything even approaching this near-blasphemous crassness. Her touch was much more subtle: she had incorporated into her portraits symbols that had been associated with the Virgin Mary, such as the rose, and had herself painted in a way reminiscent of the techniques used for pictures of the Virgin. The effect of this was twofold: as with the references to the Greek goddesses, Elizabeth could hope to bask in some of the reflected glory associated with the Virgin, and she might also hope to provide an acceptable psychological substitute for those women distressed by Protestantism's downgrading of the Virgin and the female saints.

The cult of the Virgin Queen, then, became both a source

of personal comfort for Elizabeth herself and also an important part of her attempt to minimize discontent at home and to deter potential aggression from abroad. The remaining chapters will examine the manifestations of this cult, and its interplay with the life and culture of the Elizabethan court.

III

The Court

THE court of Elizabeth had to perform a number of different functions. It had to provide a home for the Queen and her large household staff; it had to function as the seat of government; it had to be a place glittering enough and entertaining enough to act as a magnet for the high-born, high-spirited young men who might otherwise have found more dangerous outlets for their energies and enthusiasms; and it had to be sufficiently impressive and splendid to ensure that foreign ambassadors and Elizabeth's own subjects were convinced of the Queen's power and magnificence. This last function was by no means the least, for in an age that attached so much importance to symbolism and outward appearance, to possess the image of power and grandeur was in a very real sense to possess actual power and grandeur.

Until well into the late mediaeval period there had been little thought in England of an elaborate court culture. Kings for the most part had had other things to worry about; Edward I (1272–1307) had paid some attention to display, Edward III (1327–77) had had something of a cult of Arthur at his court, and Richard II (1367–99) had also been interested in court culture, but in general the royal court had been roughly similar to the households of noblemen, albeit on a grander scale. The origins of the splendid, flamboyant courts of the sixteenth century lay not in England but at the court of the Dukes of Burgundy, who ruled over a vast, sprawling collection of lands which, at the height of the Dukes' power, included not only the duchy of Burgundy as it is now but also Franche-Comté, parts of northern France, and most of what are now Holland, Belgium and Luxembourg. These unwieldy possessions had been accumulated by the Dukes as a result of a series of advantageous marriages, and they made the Dukes of Burgundy serious rivals in power, wealth and prestige to the kings of France and England.

Indeed, if there was one thing that galled the dukes it was that they were not in fact kings. One of them, Duke Philip the Good, liked to be referred to as the Grand Duke of the West, and his son Charles the Rash, the last Duke, tried very hard to persuade the Holy Roman Emperor to crown him as a king. The Emperor agreed in principle, but objected that Charles had nowhere to be king *of*—none of the lands which he ruled had ever been an independent kingdom. Charles countered this objection by looking back through old historical records and discovering that back in the early Middle Ages there had been a kingdom called Lotharingia, centred on Lorraine. There seemed no reason why Charles could not be made King of Lotharingia, except for the small problem that he did not in fact rule Lorraine. Charles at once set about putting this right. He launched a fierce campaign to seize Lorraine from its rightful Duke so that it could give its name to his proposed kingdom, but in the course of the campaign he was killed.

Since he had no son, the Duchy of Burgundy passed to his only daughter Mary, and on her marriage to the son of the Holy Roman Emperor it was absorbed into the Empire, eventually becoming one of the vast possessions inherited by Elizabeth's brother-in-law Philip of Spain. By the time of Elizabeth's reign, therefore, the once mighty Duchy of Burgundy was an international power no more. Its legacy, however, could still be felt throughout the courts of Europe.

The court of Burgundy in the fifteenth century had been the wonder of its day. It is difficult to realize this now, for Burgundy has left few lasting monuments: many of its most splendid productions were ephemeral, for while the Italian Renaissance expended its energies on paintings and sculptures and palazzi, the Dukes of Burgundy were more interested in splendid feasts, beautiful gardens, gorgeous clothes and magnificent court entertainments, all of which have of course vanished without trace. Perhaps because their lands were so distant and potentially so fragmented, lacking any logical political or geographical focus, the Dukes created around themselves a cult of personality. The first of them, for instance, Duke Philip the Bold, was born on St. Anthony's Day, and therefore always made a point of showing great devotion to St. Anthony: he named his son Anthony, and every year on St. Anthony's Day he would sacrifice to the saint as many well-fattened pigs as there were members of his family living. Also, since his wife's name was Marguerite (the French for daisy), he had all her tapestries ornamented with daisies.

Duchess Marguerite seems to have had a fondness for the pastoral life, since as well as daisies her tapestries depicted black and white ewes, shepherds and shepherdesses, her own initial entwined with the Duke's, violets, roses, forget-me-nots and hawthorn—all her underwear was also embroidered with hawthorn leaves. Duke Philip the Bold never wore the same suit of clothes twice on important occasions, and his cloaks would have elaborate clasps in such shapes as lilies, violets, peacocks, falcons, eagles, lions, bears and monkeys. His salt cellars were in the shape of mermaids, and he once gave the Duke of Anjou a golden goblet shaped like a sheaf of corn with each grain separately carved and in the bottom of the cup an enamel swan surrounded by water, lilies and leaves. The Duchess had a jewel in the form of two ewes holding a wolf, to represent gentleness triumphing over cruelty.

Ewes were not confined to the Duchess: some of her husband's clothes sported ewes with real gold bells round their necks, and he also wore clothes with embroidered swans on. His cloaks were covered with fur and his hats with jewels, and his taste in interior decoration was similarly flamboyant: one of his chambers was ornamented with branches of oak, painted red and white, in the middle of which was a painted tiger drinking from a fountain, and he also possesssed many tapestries depicting stories from the Bible, classical mythology, French history and legend, and the Arthurian cycle. Even his garden had sculptured decorations representing the shepherds and flocks of ewes of which his wife was so fond.

Duke Philip the Bold was followed by a son, a grandson and a great-grandson with similar tastes for display. His son John the Fearless besieged his uncle the Duke of Berry (who also liked display, and was accompanied wherever he went by some live bears because one of his personal symbols was a bear), and made sure that when the siege was over he acquired his uncle's best singers for his choir. John the Fearless had also inherited the family liking for the language of symbols. When he was engaged in a life-or-death struggle with his cousin, the Duke of Orléans, for the political control of France, Orléans adopted as his badge an aggressive-looking knobbly club; John the Fearless countered by adopting as his own badges a mason's level, indicating his intention to level his overmighty cousin, and a carpenter's plane, meaning that he would shave off the knobs from the Duke of Orléans' club. He even had carpenter's planes embroidered on his clothes and had small gold and silver ones made (with tiny gilded wood shavings) to give to his supporters, so that they could wear them as a badge of their allegiance to him—rather like wearing the colours of a political party or having a car bumper sticker.

When John the Fearless was murdered he was succeeded by his son, Philip the Good, the greatest of all the Dukes of Burgundy. Philip the Good's original nickname was Philip the Steady, until he let it be known that he wanted to be called Philip the Good. His reign saw the greatest of all the symbolic displays of Burgundian splendour and power: great banquets with mechanical devices, mock-castles manned by live soldiers, acrobatic displays and, on one occasion, an enormous pie containing twelve live musicians. At the Feast of the Pheasant, where everybody present took the oath to go on crusade (not to be fulfilled) and Duke Philip paid for the clothes of all present—all grey, white or black—a live pheasant appeared wearing a gold necklace studded with precious stones, and a woman representing the Church made a speech requesting the help of the assembled company to free her. But the greatest of all the celebrations of his reign when he married, as his third wife, Princess Isabella of Portugal. On that occasion a pie was served in which was a live sheep painted blue with golden horns, accompanied by an immensely large man clothed in the skin of wild animals, while the palace courtyard was filled with huge heraldic beasts from which poured wine, hippocras (a favourite drink of the period) and water.

Other entertainments included a horse caparisoned in red silk, bearing two trumpeters, back to back, riding bareback; a 12-year-old boy singing a popular song and riding on the back of a deer which had been painted white and had its horns gilded; and a monster which was half griffin and half man riding a wild boar and supporting on his back an acrobat walking on his hands. After three days of jousting Philip further announced that he was creating a new Order of Chilvalry on the model of the English Order of the Garter. It was called the Golden Fleece, after the golden fleece hunted by Jason in Greek mythology, and each knight was presented with a golden collar from which hung a golden fleece. The cost of all this was enormous, so much so that even Philip the Good, whose total income was twice that of the city of Florence and four times that of the Pope, was forced to pawn one of the golden fleece collars.

Duke Philip's tastes were no less flamboyant in other areas. In most respects he was in general an immensely dignified man, who always wore black and insisted on the observance of a rigidly formal etiquette at his court: he once threatened to run away from his own court if the Dauphin of France, who was visiting him, did not allow him to genuflect the precise number of times required by Burgundian etiquette. He did, however, have a great fondness for practical jokes, particularly ones which involved his hapless guests and courtiers getting soaked to the skin. At one of his favourite residences he had a whole gallery full of mechanical devices for playing tricks on people:

> [There was] a bridge in this room, constructed in such a way that it was possible to cause anyone walking over it to fall into the water below. There are several devices in this room which, when set off, spray large quantities of water onto the people in it, as well as six figures, more than there had been before, which soak people in different ways. In the entrance, there are eight conduits for wetting women from below and three conduits which, when people step in front of them, cover them all over with flour. When someone tries to open a certain

window, a figure appears, sprays the person with water, and shuts the window. A book of ballads lies on a desk but, when you try to read it, you are squirted with soot; if you look inside it, you can be sprayed with water. Then there is a mirror which people are invited to look at, to see themselves all white with flour; but, when they do so, they are covered with more flour. A wooden figure, which appears above a bench in the middle of the gallery, announces, at the sound of trumpets, on behalf of the duke, that everyone must leave the gallery. Those who do so are beaten by large figures holding sticks . . . and those who don't want to leave get so wet that they don't know what to do to avoid the water.*

All this may seem trivial, but such devices were seen in their time as displaying the wealth and splendour of Duke Philip, and as adding to the glory of his magnificent court—a court which even appeared to contemporaries to possess something of the lustre which they associated with the legendary court of King Arthur, for Philip, in keeping with his interest in chivalry, deliberately fostered a court culture which was based on the Arthurian legends. Burgundy, famous for its festivals, was no less famous for its tournaments, with star attractions like live chained cheetahs and real dromedaries, while the sons of the higher nobility often received Arthurian names such as Lancelot. Duke Philip did not, however, live up to the chastity of the ideal Arthurian knight: he was credited with somewhere in the region of thirty mistresses and around twenty bastards. Only one of his many children was legitimate, however, and this was his son and eventual successor, Duke Charles the Rash.

Duke Charles was a very different sort of man from his father. Although he too was obsessed with ceremony and etiquette and insisted that his courtiers observe all the rituals of court life even when on military campaigns, his military ambitions, as we have seen above, meant that his reign was short and that the power of Burgundy was effectively annihilated. Its cultural predominance, however, was already well established, so much so that when King

* Translated by Richard Vaughan, *Philip the Good* (London, 1970), p. 138, and quoted in Richard Barber, *The Penguin Guide to Medieval Europe* (Harmondsworth, Penguin: 1984), p. 237.

James III of Scotland had wanted portraits painted of himself and his wife he had sent to Burgundy for suitable bodies and background to be produced by a Burgundian painter, and had then had the picture brought to Scotland for the actual features of himself and the queen to be filled in by a less highly skilled local painter. Even more importantly, Duke Charles the Rash had married as his third wife Margaret of York, the sister of King Edward IV of England, and this meant that when an uprising in favour of his enemies the House of Lancaster had driven the Yorkist King Edward temporarily off his throne and out of England, he had gone to Burgundy to find a safe haven with his brother-in-law. There he had been tremendously impressed by the elaborateness and splendour of Burgundian court culture; and when he regained his throne the next year he immediately began to think of recreating what he had seen at his brother-in-law's court, commissioning, for instance, a pew for himself at Westminster Abbey that was an exact copy of one that he had seen in Burgundian-ruled territories.

The impression was deepened by a visit to London by Anthony, an illegitimate son of Duke Philip the Good who rejoiced in the name of the Great Bastard of Burgundy and who during his stay took part in a famously elaborate tournament which was England's first real sight of the sort of magnificent festival so popular at the Burgundian court. King Edward IV died in 1483, and two years later his brother Richard III lost his throne to the first Tudor king, Henry VII, but Henry VII married King Edward's daughter Elizabeth of York and, although he was like his granddaughter Queen Elizabeth notoriously parsimonious in most things, he did not begrudge spending money on court entertainments, because the years he had spent in his youth at the courts of France and Brittany had taught him their value in creating for the ruler a suitably splendid image.

This was particularly important to Henry VII because he was only too well aware that the legitimacy of his claim to the throne was in fact highly suspect, and that there were still members of the previous ruling dynasty, the House of York, who might well stir up rebellions and try to unseat him—as did in fact happen on two occasions during the earlier part of his reign. Henry was particularly anxious to play down his weak dynastic position by highlighting his one great strength, his Welsh parentage—the Tudors originally came from the Isle of Anglesey—which made him able to claim descent from the early princes of Wales who were popularly believed to have descended from King Arthur himself. It was to bolster this Arthurian connection that Henry christened his eldest son Arthur (although the boy unfortunately predeceased him), and Burgundian court culture, already introduced to England by Henry's father-in-law Edward IV, was the ideal vehicle for playing up Arthurian associations.

Henry, like the Burgundian dukes before him, spent lavishly on his clothes, wearing cloth-of-gold, cloth-of-silver, silks, furs and jewellery himself, and making sure that his most important courtiers did the same; he introduced the royal bodyguard of the Gentlemen Pensioners, who wore red uniforms and black caps like the Yeomen of the Guard at the Tower of London, and he clothed his other household staff in the Tudor colours of white and green. He made sure that etiquette and precedence were strictly observed, liked elaborate processions on all possible occasions, and patronized writers of courtly romances. He also believed that a court, to be suitably impressive, needed suitably impressive entertainments. Henry himself took no great pleasure in these—we are told that he would 'come, and look upon them a little, and turn away'—but he felt that they were necessary. So on feast days there would be pageants like that of St. George on Twelfth Night 1494, which was accompanied by a mock-castle and twelve dancing lords and ladies who, in the newest fashion just imported from Italy, were disguised in fancy dress and masks.

Henry was especially lavish when his great ambition was achieved by the marriage in 1501 of his eldest son Arthur to Catherine of Aragon, daughter of the powerful King Ferdinand of Aragon and Queen Isabella of Castile—a marriage which finally put the new and still insecure dynasty of the Tudors on a footing with the other royal families of Europe. A tournament was held in front of Westminster

Hall with a 'tree of chivalry' on which the contestants could hang their shields, and the knights who came to fight made particularly splendid entrances: one was hidden inside a dragon which was led by a giant, one came on a wagon decorated to look like a ship with sailors on board firing cannon, and one on a wagon disguised as a grassy mountain. The evening entertainment included acrobatic displays, music, dancing and many splendid allegorical pageants, including one where mermaids led in sea-horses, with boys inside them singing, which pulled behind them a tower with knights on the ground floor and ladies above them: one where ladies in disguise occupied a moated castle which was attacked by knights in a sailing ship who climbed a ladder, carried off the ladies, and then danced with them on a 'mountain' which had also been erected in the hall; and one in which twelve ladies were brought into the hall in a huge transparent lantern to dance with twelve gentlemen concealed in an arbour. Henry was determined that his court should not be shown up in the eyes of the daughter of Ferdinand and Isabella. In fact, the marriage was soon followed by mourning when young Arthur fell ill and died, and not long afterwards he was followed to the grave by his mother, Queen Elizabeth of York, who had never really recovered from his death; and after the deaths of his wife and son Henry VII lost his appetite for festivals and ceremonies, so that for the last few years of his reign the court was quiet. The pattern had been established, however, and under Henry VII's son and successor, Henry VIII, court entertainments were soon revived again.

Henry VII in his last years had grown even closer with money than before, and so when Henry VIII came to the throne he inherited what at first appeared to be a boundless amount of wealth which, unlike his father, he was determined to spend. Almost his first action as King was to marry his brother's widow, Catherine of Aragon, and in the early days of their marriage life was one long party, with Henry and his gentlemen frequently bursting into Catherine's apartments in various outlandish disguises and forcing Catherine and her ladies to dance with them before removing their masks to show who they were—at which the obliging Catherine never failed to be suitably amazed. When Catherine's first child was born the delighted Henry held a tournament where he himself, under the name of 'Coeur loyal'—loyal heart—participated. He and three companions entered on a wagon decorated as a forest, with hills and valleys and, in the middle, a gold castle in which sat a man who was making a garland of roses for the new Prince of Wales. The wagon was drawn by men dressed as a lion and an antelope. Henry wore a costume studded with his own and the Queen's initials in gold thread—until the sight unfortunately proved too much for the watching crowd, who mobbed him and left him and his courtiers stripped almost naked.

Unfortunately the baby prince soon died, but that was not the end of festivities at court. At Greenwich Palace on New Year's Eve, 1512, a castle called le Fortresse dangerous was carried into the hall, complete with towers, gates, a dungeon and guns. In it were six ladies in russet and gold, who were promptly besieged by Henry and five of his gentlemen until they agreed to dance with them. Later in the reign, at the coronation of Henry's second wife, Queen Anne Boleyn, wine flowed free in the streets.

Nothing, however, could eclipse the splendours of the Field of the Cloth of Gold, a meeting between Henry VIII and King Francis I of France, who at 26 was only three years younger than Henry's 29, was said to be just as handsome as Henry and no less successful with women, and was therefore regarded by Henry as a dangerous rival for the position of the most splendid king in Europe (Henry was much more favourably disposed towards the Emperor Charles V, who with his jutting Habsburg jaw and his unimpressive physique made Henry look all the better by contrast). The Field of the Cloth of Gold was held near Calais in June 1520 and attended by 6,000 people in all. With each side determined not to be outdone by the other, the festivities were some of the most splendid ever seen, with the occasion taking its name from the amount of cloth-of-gold in evidence.

The tent which accommodated King Francis during his stay

was 120 feet high, made from canvas covered with cloth-of-gold and fleur-de-lys and topped with a life-size statue of St. Michael. Its windows were made of thin cotton. There was also a round banqueting house made of canvas painted to look like brick with a blue roof covered with stars and planets painted in gold, but this had to be dismantled after four days because of the unseasonable wind and rain. Henry, not to be outdone, had erected a temporary palace made of wood painted to look like brick, with fountains in the courtyard in the shapes of Cupid and Bacchus and separate conduits for red wine, white wine and claret, all of which ran free. 820 other tents housed the remaining people present. There were many tournaments, pageants and masques where the participants all appeared in elaborate allegorical costumes, and at the banquets there was said to be so much food that people were choking. Henry was served by the French with what were known as 'subtleties', sugar concoctions in the shape of animals, people or buildings; on this occasion there were leopards (the royal beast of England), ermines and salamanders (the personal symbol of Francis I). The English brought with them, for the thirteen days that the occasion lasted, 76,518 litres of wine, 156,960 litres of beer and, rather incongruously, 200 apples: a statistic which indicates something about the unhealthiness of the contemporary diet.

This, then, was the court culture inherited by Elizabeth. As already suggested, its purpose was something rather more than mere frivolity. It served to display the wealth and power of the ruler; and it also made the court an exciting place to be. Anyone who aspired to power would both need and want to come to court, and once they were there Elizabeth could keep an eye on them, know what they were doing, and prevent possible trouble at the earliest possible moment.

In the centuries before the Tudors came to the throne the Kings of England had had considerable trouble controlling the landed classes; whenever there was a weak King or a period of unrest all too many people who could afford to do so had seized the opportunity to break the law by putting up unlicensed castles, from the safety of which they could hope to defy the royal authority, and no Tudor could afford to forget that not so very long ago, in 1485, the nobility of England had rallied behind a pretender to the throne and ousted the ruling King, Richard III. It was true that in that instance the pretender had in fact been Henry Tudor, who as Henry VII had become the first Tudor king, but the Tudors were only too well aware that what could work in their favour could also work against them.

One traditional and successful way of keeping the nobles too busy to think about rebellion had been to start a war, which would cause the nation to forget any internal disagreements by uniting it against a common enemy, just as in Shakespeare's *Henry IV, Part 2* the dying King Henry IV advises his son, the future Henry V, that in order to ensure peace at home he should 'busy giddy minds/ With foreign quarrels' (IV, 5, 214). Although Elizabeth did in fact achieve this when war with Spain was thrust on her by the arrival of the Armada, wars cost money, and since Elizabeth was throughout her reign immensely parsimonious this was therefore not an attractive solution. Instead she concentrated on luring young men to court and, once they had arrived, keeping them there for as long as possible.

Her natural tendency to like to have them around her was dramatically strengthened when one of the most promising of them, Sir Philip Sidney, was mortally wounded at the battle of Zutphen, in the Netherlands, where Elizabeth's troops were helping the Protestant Dutch to fight their repressively Catholic Spanish overlords. As he lay injured Sidney had insisted on handing his water bottle to another wounded soldier, with the words 'Thy necessity is yet greater than mine', and the nobility of his death, together with the brilliant promise he had shown in the literary and diplomatic fields, made him into a national hero. However, Elizabeth drew from his death the lesson that war and expeditions were something which could deprive her at best temporarily, and at worst permanently, of the company of the handsome young men whom she so loved to have about her. When another favourite, Sir Charles Blount, absconded to join the army, Elizabeth ordered the commander of the forces to return him at once, and when Blount duly arrived home she berated him:

Serve me so once more, and I will lay you fast enough for running. You will never leave it until you are knocked on the head, as that inconsiderate fellow Sidney was. You shall go when I send you, and in the meantime see that you lodge in the Court, where you may follow your book, read and discourse of the wars.

When the chief favourite of her later years, the Earl of Essex, similarly joined the fleet which had been sent to help the Portuguese, who were at war with England's enemy Spain, the letters which Elizabeth sent after him were so explosive that Sir Francis Drake, who was in charge of the English ships, sent him straight home again.

The reason for Sidney's death had in fact been that he had gone out to fight, on the morning he was wounded, without putting on the protective thigh-pieces which formed part of a suit of his armour. He was hit in the thigh, and the wound festered, eventually proving mortal. One of the reasons for Sidney's decision to leave off his thigh-pieces together might well have been that he, like so many young gentlemen about the court, could have been influenced by the ideas about the sort of behaviour appropriate to a courtier which had gained considerable currency since the publication in Italian of Castiglione's *The Courtier* and its translation into English by Sir Thomas Hoby. This book, more than any other piece of writing, conveys the feel of a Renaissance court and the sort of life led by courtiers, permanently on display and paying intense attention to cultivating and maintaining a suitable public image. Castiglione insists that one of the most important qualities for a courtier is what he terms *sprezzatura*, which can perhaps best be translated as nonchalance: the courtier must be superbly good at everything while looking as though he puts no effort into it whatsoever. When he fights battles, he must make sure his commanding officer sees any feats of bravery he may perform; conversely, if he needs to practise anything in order to be good at it, he must make sure that he does this where nobody can catch him at it; and he must at all times keep an eye open to check on the effect he is producing. An example of these principles put into practice comes from Sir John Harington, a court wit and a godson of the Queen:

We go brave in apparel that we may be taken for better men than we be; we use much bumbastings and quiltings to seem fitter formed, better shouldered, smaller waisted, fuller thighed than we are; we barbe (trim our beards) and shave often to seem younger than we are; we use perfumes both inward and outward to seem sweeter than we be; we use courteous salutations to seem kinder than we be; and sometimes graver and godly communications, to seem wiser than we be.

Along with this interest in one's image there naturally went an interest in fashion, for both men and women. While the ruffs of the women became larger and stiffer, thanks to the technique of starching imported from Holland, men were resplendent in padded trunk-hose, elaborate velvet doublets, plumed hats, silk stockings (Elizabeth was notoriously quick to notice a well-shaped leg on a man, and the dances popular at court gave men many opportunities to leap and caper and show their legs to best advantage) and cloaks of various colours and fabrics, velvet and taffeta being especially popular. Cloaks could be slashed, to show the rich lining underneath, embroidered, and ornamented with glass, tassels, or even jewels such as pearls.

But the most splendid clothes at court were, of course, those worn by the Queen herself. Elizabeth's collection of clothes and jewels was vast: by the end of her reign she had some hundreds of dresses and 125 petticoats. Her favourite colours were black and white, but she was also fond of an orange tawny colour which went well with her hair and wore many other colours, too, though she was not fond of blue, green or yellow. Wherever she went she was set off by her Maids of Honour, who by the end of the reign were always dressed in silver and white, with Elizabeth often forsaking the black and white of her middle years to join them in the same colours.

All Elizabeth's dresses tended to be very highly decorated, often with motifs which were important for their symbolic as well as their ornamental properties, such as rainbows (the sign of peace, since a rainbow was God's covenant after the Flood that his anger against men was now appeased), serpents (symbols of wisdom), pillars (associated with the idea of empire), symbolic animals, birds, fruit and flowers such as roses (associated with perfection and with the Virgin Mary) and pansies, indicating thought, and other devices like insects, swords, pineapple trees, fish, cobwebs (perhaps indicative of the industry associated with the spider), lions, whales, dragons (possibly because of her Welsh connections), seas with clouds and rainbows, the Nine Muses (at a court masque late in the reign eight of Elizabeth's ladies appeared as eight of the Nine Muses come to seek the Queen, their lost sister), eyes and ears to show that she heard and saw everything, and flames, possibly representing the passion she inspired in her admirers: to those acquainted with the meaning of their symbols, Elizabeth's dresses spoke as clearly as words of her power, her virtues, and her wisdom.

Many dresses were still further adorned with jewels or pearls (sometimes artificial) sewn onto them, or by gold braid. On one occasion Bishop Aylmer (the same bishop who had obligingly volunteered to act as a guinea-pig for the Queen by having one of his own teeth pulled out before hers was extracted) mentioned in a sermon 'the vanity of decking the body too finely'. Elizabeth was furious, and her godson, the writer and wit Sir John Harington, suggested that if the bishop had ever paid a visit to Her Majesty's wardrobe, he would have chosen another text.

Even her household furniture contained reminders of her rank and status: her walnut bed, which could be dismantled to travel with her as she moved from residence to residence, was decorated with heraldic beasts and with the ostrich feathers which were associated with the principality of Wales from which her family came and of which she herself had once been Princess. Another bed was made of 'woods of different colours, with quilts of silk, velvet, gold and silver embroidery' and hangings of 'Indian work of silk painted on one side', and there was a table completely covered with silver. She had also inherited from her father, Henry VIII, the treasures that had been amassed at Hampton Court by the King's powerful minister Wolsey, which included a twenty-eight foot long velvet table cover which reached to the ground and was covered with pearls 'as large as peas',

Persian tapestries, and other tapestries with the royal arms and real diamonds woven into them. There were also items for the Queen to use in her favoured recreations of playing games and making music: an ebony draughts board, an ivory chess board and a backgammon table where the dice were made of silver and the pieces were perfumed and decorated with heraldic crests; and a large collection of musical instruments.

No less splendid was Elizabeth's jewellery collection, which grew larger every year thanks to the custom of the court exchanging gifts every New Year (there were no Christmas presents given at this period). Although the Queen gave presents in exchange, they were never equivalent in value to the ones she received. One of the ways in which Elizabeth's carefulness with money showed itself was in her extreme fondness for presents: towards the end of her reign one of her progresses travelled less far than had been expected, and when she returned home Elizabeth was so annoyed to find that people whom she had not managed to visit had been expecting her and had had presents in readiness for her that the next year she repeated her route but made sure that this time she travelled further along it, to pick up the presents she had missed the year before! She also saw to it that her assistance to Dom Antonio, the pretender to the throne of Portugal, was recompensed by his family jewels, and the turmoil of emotion she felt after she had finally agreed to execute her cousin Mary, Queen of Scots, did not stop her from acquiring the late Queen's famous black pearls.

Thanks to practices such as these, her collection of precious objects was immense: a visiting Italian duke reported to his wife that she wore so many jewels he did not know how she could carry them. She had jewels in the shape of moons (one of the names given to her by her courtiers was Cynthia, the goddess of the moon), suns, flowers, fish, gods and goddesses. There was a dolphin made of gold and rubies, a greyhound (one of the heraldic beasts of the Tudors) made of gold and with a diamond collar, a white enamel pendant showing Adam and Eve, a mermaid made of gold and diamonds and, intriguingly, a gold jewel with diamonds and pearls which showed a cat playing with some mice. There were bracelets, ear-rings and hair ornaments. There were jewels in the shape of pelicans, which were supposed to feed their young by tearing strips of flesh from their own breasts: they had therefore become symbols of Christ, who gave His own body and blood to be eaten at the Communion service, and they were appropriate symbols for Elizabeth both in view of her liking for surrounding herself with images with religious connotations and also because as a queen she could be supposed to sacrifice herself for her country. There were phoenixes, too: they were popularly believed to burn themselves to death on fires from the ashes of which they then arose again renewed, and therefore were another bird which was associated with Christ, since they too underwent a resurrection. Again this religious symbolism made the phoenix appropriate for the cult of Elizabeth, and it also provided a comforting psychological counterweight to the visible fact that Elizabeth was in fact an ageing, childless woman by suggesting that the majesty which she embodied would not perish but somehow be mystically renewed. This in turn tied in with the contemporary theory of the ruler having not one but two bodies: one the body of flesh and blood which would die and decay like everyone else's; the other an intangible essence which would almost magically be transmitted to the ruler's successor, just as the phoenix was born again.

As well as jewels, Elizabeth would be given as presents other forms of finery, such as fans made of ostrich feathers or decorated with jewels or symbolic devices—one had two serpents, signifying wisdom, twining round the handle, and another bore a bear and ragged staff, the family crest of her long-time favourite, the Earl of Leicester—a wise present to give because it meant that every time the Queen used the fan she and everyone who saw it would be reminded of him; tiny, exquisitely-embroidered handkerchiefs, some of them made of cloth-of-gold or cloth-of-silver; cushions, often embroidered and including one covered with gold and seed pearls, because she was fond of sitting on the floor; embroidered gloves; and bags of lavender and other herbs to hang around her clothes when they were not being worn. One particularly successful New Year's gift, very early in the reign, was a pair of silk stockings, with which Elizabeth was so delighted that she vowed she would never wear cloth stockings again. And, last but not least, there was a so-called unicorn's horn, which had been brought back from a voyage to Florida, was valued at £100,000 and was also hung among her dresses as it was believed to act as a preventative against poison, which, it was believed in the sixteenth century, could be applied to clothes. A unicorn's horn was also a particularly appropriate possession for a Virgin Queen since unicorns could traditionally be caught only if a virgin was present: she must sit down in a clearing in the forest and the unicorn would then come and lay his head in her lap, upon which the hunter would be able to trap or kill him. Because of this legend the unicorn became yet another symbol for Christ, who would be born of no mother but a virgin, and so even the furnishings of Elizabeth's wardrobe provided yet another opportunity for her to enhance her image by surrounding herself with religious symbolism. In the Elizabethan court, even the most minor aspects of court life all had to reflect the power and glory of the sun around whom it revolved.

IV

The Courtiers

FOR much the greater part of Elizabeth's reign the man at court with most real power was William Cecil. The Cecils were, like the Tudors, a Welsh family: their name had originally been Sisyllt, but when they came to England they had changed it to Cecil (pronounced something like Sissil), which had the double advantage of being at once more easily pronounced by English people and of recalling the fame and eminence of the great ancient Roman family of the Caecilii. Adopting Roman names in this way was not unknown in the period: there was even a knight at court who rejoiced in the name of Sir Julius Caesar. By calling themselves after an important Roman family the Cecils intended to enhance their own status by association; behind their action lay much the same principle as that of inviting a famous sporting or cinema personality to appear in an advert for something with which he has no connection, but which can still benefit by being associated with him.

The Elizabethan world-view had, moreover, developed out of the mediaeval world-view, which loved to see things in terms of patterns, correspondences and what were called 'types', things which matched other things. This can be easily seen in a mediaeval church where the original sculpture and stained glass remain intact, such as Chartres Cathedral, where the entire north side of the church is given over to figures from the Old Testament who are implicitly compared with the figures from the New Testament on the south side. The Old Testament figures were thought of as 'types'—figures who correspond to each other or fulfilled the same purpose as each other—of the New Testament ones: Elijah was a type of John the Baptist; Jonah, who emerged from the stomach of a whale, was a type of Christ who descended into Hell to free the righteous there and returned; Moses, who gave the Old Law, was another type of Christ, who gave the New Law; Mary, on the other hand, was an antitype, or reversal of Eve—a point that the middle ages liked to emphasize by referring to Eve by her Latin name of Eva and to Mary as the Ave, after the greeting uttered to her by the angel Gabriel, 'Ave Maria'. ('Ave' is a direct reversal of 'Eva', since the letters are the same only running in different directions, and the mediaeval mind saw this as a neat demonstration of the way in which Mary was in fact the reverse of Eve. A popular mediaeval carol contains the line 'Ave fit ex Eva', which means 'Ave [the Virgin Mary] comes out of Eva'.)

This mediaeval tendency to see the world in terms of patterns and types was reinforced by the new philosophy of neo-Platonism which was gradually beginning to filter out of Italy. Plato had been one of the most important philosophers of the classical world, and one of his most influential tenets had been that the things which we see on earth are in fact vague and unsatisfactory reflections of an ideal version of that object which exists in the heavens. To this ideal version Plato gave the name of an Idea or a Form. This idea was resurrected and further expounded in Italy, in the late fifteenth century, by the famous scholar Marsilio Ficino, a humanist—a student of the new learning of the Renaissance—who was the friend and tutor of the great Lorenzo de' Medici, called the Magnificent, effective ruler of Florence and a great patron of learning and the arts. Another figure important in the spread of neo-Platonism had been Giovanni Pico della Mirandola, whose work had been translated into English.

Neo-Platonic ideas were complex and difficult, and their full impact was not felt in England until well into the next century, when the French wife of King Charles I, Henrietta Maria, introduced them to the English court, but the stress on things on earth as images of things in the heavens was so congenial to existing habits of thinking that it further reinforced the Elizabethan idea that, in some sense, the image or outward appearance of a thing had a fundamental correspondence with the nature of the thing itself. Of course the Elizabethans were well aware that they were worrying exceptions to this rule—they knew as well as anybody that an ugly body may contain a pleasant person and vice versa— but there was nevertheless a magnetic attraction to the belief that appearances correspond with reality. It is perhaps the conflict between the strength of this belief, and the fact that experience often contradicted it, that is partly responsible for the urgency with which Shakespeare in so many of his plays explores the relationship between seeming and being. At all events, there was in Elizabethan society as strong a perception as amongst any group of political image-makers that the image can be fundamentally important, underpinned by a feeling that if image and reality corresponded, then to alter the image might be in some sense to bring the reality into line with it. In the case of the Cecil family, then, the link between their name and that of the great Roman family served more than one purpose. It indicated that they were possessed of classical scholarship, which was becoming increasingly a mark of status; and it might also have the effect not only of enhancing their image but of actually elevating their status.

Their name might even manage to suggest that they were in fact descendants of the Caecilii, and in the Elizabethan period there was immense interest in family history and genealogy: everyone with any claim to respectability or status was anxious to be able to produce the most impressive family tree possible, and most people did not mind forging one if they needed to. The heralds, the people responsible for establishing family histories, did a thriving trade in producing increasingly grand and unlikely genealogies for their clients, culminating in the family tree produced for Elizabeth, where her descent was proudly traced back through King Arthur and the Trojan Brutus, the legendary founder of Britain, to Noah and finally to no less a personage than Adam himself (though who, it might be asked, does *not* descend from Adam?). Thus it would do the Cecils no harm if their name were taken to indicate a long and distinguished family tree.

The first of the family to come to court had been William Cecil's grandfather David, who, like so many Welshmen, had rallied behind the Welsh Henry Tudor when, in 1485, he had marched to Bosworth Field to make his bid for the crown. After Henry had won the Battle of Bosworth and ascended the throne as King Henry VII, Henry made David Cecil one of his newly-established Yeomen of the Guard, in which service David acquired enough money to make the most profitable of all Elizabethan investments: he bought land, in this case near Stamford, where in due course he became both Mayor and M.P. He also got his son Richard placed first as a page to King Henry VIII and then as a groom of the Privy Chamber. The family was firmly set for success, which came in the next generation with Richard's son William.

William Cecil's career at court began, like his father's, as a page, after which he went to Cambridge, where he early showed signs of the inventiveness which was to stand him in such good stead later in his career. One night he lost a bet on which he had staked everything he owned, including his books and his bedding. He soon, however, thought of a way of getting out of this dire situation. In the middle of the night he drilled a hole above the head of the bed of the man who had won his money, and he spoke through it in sepulchral tones, telling his victim to forswear gambling or be damned for ever. Taking this as a divine warning, the man promptly cancelled Cecil's debt to him.

After his Cambridge days, William went to court, where his real training began in the reign of Elizabeth's half-brother King Edward VI, when he was taken into the service of the powerful Duke of Somerset, the King's uncle and Lord Protector of the realm. This took Cecil on Somerset's campaigns against the Scots, where, although not a combatant, he nearly fell victim to a stray bullet. That and what he saw of the ravages of the campaign left him with a profound dislike of war, which in later years made him thoroughly in agreement with Elizabeth's anti-war policy. Soon after this the Duke of Somerset was ousted from power by the Duke of Northumberland and both he and Cecil were sent to the Tower. The Duke was executed, but Cecil, having learned a useful lesson in the dangers of politics, was soon out again and working for Northumberland.

Soon he found himself in danger yet again. Northumberland knew that King Edward VI, ill with tuberculosis, had not long to live, and that the succession of his Catholic half-sister Mary Tudor would mean that Edward's Protestant appointees would all fall from power; and he therefore planned to marry Lady Jane Grey, who had a claim to the throne, to his own son and install them as King and Queen. He demanded that all his servants should sign a paper agreeing to this. Cecil, although in fear of his life, refused to sign until the King himself ordered him to do so, showing that he had principles as well as brains. Even Queen Mary, when she had crushed the rebellion in favour of Lady Jane Grey and acceded to the throne, pardoned him on the grounds that he had obeyed the orders of the King and was an honest man.

Throughout Mary's reign Cecil lay low, though he, like Elizabeth herself, agreed to attend Mass in public while remaining a Protestant in private—the sort of outward conformity which they were both later to urge to Catholics. He was also looking after the estates of the Princess Elizabeth, and during this period they continued to exchange messages. When Mary died and Elizabeth became Queen, she at once appointed Cecil her chief minister.

Cecil was immensely efficient, experienced in government, loyal, honest, intelligent and far-seeing. Even Elizabeth's cousin Mary, Queen of Scots, although knowing that Cecil was one of the people who was trying to persuade Elizabeth to execute her, said that she envied her cousin for having so wise and trustworthy a servant. Elizabeth knew what he was worth and valued him immensely: knowing that he suffered terribly from gout, she once interrupted an oration at Oxford to ask that a stool be brought for him; in his last illness she fed him with her own hand, with a spoon; and after his death she could never hear his name mentioned without crying. Nor was the gratitude of his Queen Cecil's only reward. He did so well out of the profits of his various offices that he was able to build two of the greatest houses of the age, Burghley and Theobalds (which no longer stands). He and the Queen evolved an immensely successful working partnership which steered the country through deeply hazardous waters with a very large degree of success. Even Cecil, however, did not always find life at court easy. He was often reduced almost to despair by Elizabeth's absolute inability to make up her mind, and he was sometimes on the receiving end of her notorious Tudor temper.

The worst crisis in their relationship came over the execution of Mary, Queen of Scots. The Queen of Scots had, one way or another, been causing trouble to England from almost the moment of her birth. When she was one week old, her father had died, leaving her, his only legitimate child, Queen of a country that was already experiencing religious upheaval with the advent of Protestantism and had been devastated by the recent victory in which the English had virtually annihilated the Scottish army and had left the country ripe for invasion. King Henry VIII had been determined to rid England once and for all of a hostile northern neighbour by incorporating Scotland into England through the marriage of the baby Mary to his son, the future Edward VI.

The Scots, however, had had other ideas. They did not wish to see their country subsumed into England and had sent their baby Queen to the safety of France, Scotland's traditional ally against England and the home of Mary's mother. Mary had been brought up at the French court—where she had, of course, been educated as a Catholic—and at the age of 16 had been married to the Dauphin Francis, the heir to the throne of France. Further, her new father-in-law, King Henry II of France, had taken the opportunity to declare that his daughter-in-law was not only Queen of Scotland and future Queen of France, but also rightful heir to the throne of England. This was because the King of France, like other Catholics, had always refused to recognize the legality of Henry VIII's divorce from Catherine of Aragon and, consequently, that of his subsequent marriage to Elizabeth's mother Anne Boleyn, and Elizabeth, therefore, was, in their eyes, a bastard and as such incapable of succeeding to the throne of England.

The King of France had therefore ordered that the young Mary should display not only her own royal arms of Scotland and the royal arms of France, but the arms of England too. Elizabeth was understandably furious at this insult and, not being prepared to regard Mary's youth as an excuse, blamed her for it as much as the King of France. In any case, even if Elizabeth had wanted to bear a grudge against the King of France, she could not have done so for long. Soon after the marriage of Mary to his son the King was dead, accidentally hit in the eye by a lance which pierced his helmet during a joust, thus eerily fulfilling the prophecy of the astrologer Nostradamus, on whom his wife Queen Catherine de' Medici placed so much reliance, that the lion (Henry) would be killed in its golden cage (his gilt helmet).

The death of her father-in-law made Mary, already Queen of Scotland, Queen of France as well. Such an accumulation of power was a threat to both Spain, the neighbour of France, and England, the neighbour of Scotland; but it did not last long. Within a year Mary's husband King Francis II, still only 16, was dead from an immensely painful abscess in his ear, and the young Queen was a widow. Now Mary discovered to her cost how foolish she had been when, as a young, beautiful and confident ruling Queen, she had made jokes about the fact that her mother-in-law, Queen Catherine de' Medici, was descended not from royalty but from the Italian banking family of the Medici. Queen Catherine had never forgiven the insult, and now she was Regent for the new King, her son King Charles IX. Quickly forestalling the inclination shown by the boy-king to marry Mary, whom he had always liked, Queen Catherine made it plain to her former daughter-in-law that she was no longer welcome in France and must return to her own country of Scotland.

Scotland had been ruled for Mary in her absence by her mother, the Dowager Queen Marie of Guise, but her mother had died not long before and Mary had now no real ties with Scotland except that, by accident of birth, she was its Queen. For a Catholic brought up at the splendid court of France the austerity of Scotland, where the dominant religious influence was the Calvinist John Knox, must have been a grim prospect. Mary made a valiant effort to rule her country, however, and her reign was, unusually for the time, marked by a genuine search for tolerance, wherever possible, in religious affairs. But the obstacles facing her were immense—many parts of Scotland were almost lawless, and the country had never had a female ruler before—and her two disastrous marriages, first to her cousin Lord Darnley and then, after his death, to the man who had almost certainly murdered him, the Earl of Bothwell, eventually led to her imprisonment and enforced abdication.

Throughout her life, however, Mary showed an extraordinary capacity to captivate those who came into contact with her or even heard about her, and she soon found a way of winning over one of her jailers and escaping from her captivity. Then she made the biggest mistake of her life. Instead of trying to make for France, the country which she knew so well and where as a Dowager Queen she still had estates and would have been respected and maintained in comfort for the rest of her life, she decided to cross the border with England and throw herself on the mercy of her cousin Queen Elizabeth.

This surprise move threw Elizabeth into an agonizing dilemma. Mary, when she came to England, had relied on two things: in the first place she and Elizabeth were cousins—Elizabeth's grandfather, King Henry VII, had been Mary's great-grandfather—and in the second place they shared the bond of both being anointed Queens. Mary thought that both these things would weigh heavily with Elizabeth, and to a great extent she was right. Elizabeth might have no particular objection to killing a relative (she would later, for reasons of state, sign the death warrant of her cousin on her mother's side, the Duke of Norfolk, although she did try hard beforehand to save him); but she would be very deeply reluctant to kill an anointed Queen, because to do so would let people see that killing a monarch, which ideally ought to be unthinkable, was something that could in fact be done, and that was something that could all too easily rebound on Elizabeth herself. On the other hand, to let Mary live was almost equally uncomfortable for Elizabeth. She could not possibly be allowed to return to Scotland, since it was vital for England's security that the unusually good relations which the country was currently enjoying with Scotland—ruled by Protestant regents for Mary's son James—should not be disturbed. England was already threatened by Catholic France and Spain; while

70

Scotland stayed Protestant, however, they were safe from that quarter. It would be madness to allow the Catholic Mary to return there.

The only alternative, therefore, was to keep her in prison in England. But this solution had drawbacks of its own. Prisoners can be rescued, and there were still plenty of people in England and abroad who would dearly love to see Catholicism restored in the country; and nothing would bring this about more quickly than to assassinate Elizabeth and put Mary on the English throne in her place. Elizabeth's ministers tried to persuade her that as long as Mary was still alive she would always be a focus for this type of Catholic plot, and indeed during Mary's nineteen years of imprisonment enough such plots were made to justify their fears. Still, however, Elizabeth would not agree to Mary's execution. Instead she adopted the strategy which her father had used when he wanted to see the end of Catherine of Aragon, moving Mary to increasingly unhealthy places and restricting her exercise in the hope that she would fall ill and die of natural causes. But although Mary's health was undermined (she put on weight and, like Elizabeth, lost her hair), she obstinately refused to die.

The true story of how the crisis was eventually resolved will probably never be clear. Yet another plot to kill Elizabeth and put Mary on the throne was 'discovered', although the Elizabethan secret service had in fact known of it for some time and had been allowing it to continue to gather evidence against the plotters. Mary was tried for treason, and although she refused to acknowledge the legality of the court or its power to judge the sovereign Queen of another country, a death warrant was prepared for her. Preparing the warrant, however, was one matter; getting Elizabeth to sign it was something altogether different. For more than three months she hesitated to sign the piece of paper which would condemn a fellow Queen to be executed, although she more than once privately sounded out various people about their willingness to assassinate Mary in secret.

Then, at last, the document was signed, Mary was executed—and Elizabeth at once raised an outcry, claiming that she had never knowingly signed the warrant and that it must have been slipped in with other papers awaiting her signature without her noticing. The secretary responsible, William Davison, complained that this was simply not true: Elizabeth had signed the warrant knowingly, although she had shown signs of second thoughts and her whole behaviour at the time had been erratic and confusing. No one can know the truth. Elizabeth's feelings were probably so deeply divided on the matter that the only way for her to cope with her conflicting emotions and her sense of guilt may have been for her to shift her sense of responsibility onto someone else, and a charitable interpretation could argue that she might even have succeeded in convincing herself that she was not to blame and had been tricked. At all events, the wretched Davison spent a year in the Tower and never worked for her again; and even Cecil, normally so high in Elizabeth's favour, was kept away from court for four months before Elizabeth either forgave him or discovered that she could no longer manage without him.

The Mary, Queen of Scots affair indicates both the very real dangers of Elizabeth's situation, and the difficulties that had to be negotiated by those who served her and lived at her court. The precariousness of her actual position made her all the more anxious to bolster her status in the eyes of the world by magnificent display and a splendid court; the splendours of the court in turn attracted to her numerous courtiers, but glitter and grandeur was not all they found at court. The difficulties with which the Queen was beset tried her nerves and the loneliness of her position as a Virgin Queen (perhaps coupled with the early loss of her mother and the insecurity of her childhood) left her craving affection and comfort. For this the only available source was her courtiers, and towards them Elizabeth could be both very emotionally demanding, and very resentful when her demands were not met. Life at court might be glamorous, but it could also, as Davison and Cecil discovered on the occasion of Mary, Queen of Scots' execution, be a minefield.

The people who, on a day-to-day basis, were closest of all to Elizabeth, and who therefore came in for more than ordinary shares of both her smiles and her anger, were the

Maids of Honour. The Maids of Honour changed throughout the reign as successive girls left to marry or, occasionally, died, but they were always girls from good families (sometimes, indeed, two or even three generations of the same family can be found serving as Maids of Honour over the course of Elizabeth's long reign), clever and well-educated enough to be able to provide intelligent companionship for the Queen (herself no mean scholar) and pretty enough to form an attractive backdrop to her on important occasions. Elizabeth, even when she grew older, never showed any signs of realizing that the good looks of some of these girls might in fact be regarded less as setting off her own and more as rivalling them: a tactful French visitor illustrated perfectly the idea of what the Maids of Honour should be when, asked by the Queen what he thought of them, he proclaimed himself unable 'to judge stars in the presence of the sun'. Unfortunately, though, the French visitor's apparent lack of susceptibility to the charms of the Maids of Honour was not shared by everyone at court, and this was to be the cause of a great deal of trouble at various times in the reign.

Elizabeth's attitude to the marriage of her Maids of Honour was, like her attitude to the possibility of marriage for herself, wildly variable. Sometimes, especially when the marriage was a suitable one and when the bride-to-be proposed staying in her service after the wedding, she would be perfectly amenable; at other times, particularly if the young man was one of her own favourites or if the courtship had been conducted in secret, she would react with terrifying fury and sometimes even violence; occasionally her attitude was somewhere in between these two extremes, as with the marriage of her Maid of Honour Anne Russell to Lord Herbert in 1600, where she not only gave her consent to the marriage but even promised to attend it, but then put off for so long fixing a day which would be convenient for her that the bride's mother—who was, fortunately, a fearless and determined woman—had to go and confront her about it. What was particularly unfortunate was that the fact that the Queen was known to react badly to some marriages, especially secret ones, created a vicious circle in which young couples who were too nervous to ask for her permission or who felt that they would probably not receive it would marry in secret—only to face an even greater storm of wrath since their secret, in the days before birth control, was inevitably discovered.

The tradition of secret marriages began early in the reign. Elizabeth's first group of Maids of Honour included Lady Catherine Grey, the younger sister of Lady Jane Grey, who had been used as a pawn in the Duke of Northumberland's plan to prevent the Catholic Mary Tudor from succeeding to the throne, and who had lost her head for it. The death of her elder sister had been a terrible lesson for Lady Catherine in the dangers attached to her position as a great-niece of Henry VIII, and as a possible heir to the English crown if anything should happen to Elizabeth. Mary Tudor's widower, King Philip II of Spain, had already plotted to kidnap Lady Catherine, marry her to his unstable son Don Carlos, and then launch an invasion of England to depose Elizabeth and put them on the throne; and Lady Catherine's position was made still more difficult by the fact that Elizabeth was only too well aware that she represented a potential threat and that people might intrigue with Lady Catherine as they always did around the heir to the throne and just as they had intrigued around Elizabeth herself in her sister Mary's reign. Lady Catherine knew that Elizabeth consequently did not like her and would be very unlikely ever to allow her to marry, since if Lady Catherine were to produce a son it would make her look like an even better candidate for the succession.

But even Elizabeth could not stop people from falling in love. One of the other Maids of Honour was Lady Jane Seymour, whose aunt had been Queen Jane Seymour and whose father, the Duke of Somerset, had therefore been the uncle of King Edward VI. For a brief period during the reign of King Edward the Duke of Somerset had been Lord Protector of the Realm, but then he had been toppled by his enemy the Duke of Northumberland and had eventually been beheaded. If her father had not fallen from power, Lady Jane Seymour might perhaps have been Queen of England, since her father had been scheming to marry her to her cousin the young King Edward; but now she was a Maid of Honour like her friend Lady Catherine. Lady Jane was notable among the Maids of Honour for her scholarship, but unfortunately she was equally notable for her frequent bouts of ill-health. After one of these she was sent to the home of her widowed mother, which, being in the country, was thought to be better suited to an invalid than the unhealthy air of the town, and her friend Lady Catherine Grey went too, to keep her company. But they were not the only people staying with the widowed Duchess: her son Edward, the Earl of Hertford, was there too. When Lady Catherine and he had been children the Earl's father, the Duke of Somerset, and Lady Catherine's father, the Duke of Suffolk, had planned to marry them to one another, but the plan had lapsed when the Duke of Somerset fell from power. Now, however, the Earl and Lady Catherine discovered how very glad they would have been if that plan had been carried out, for they rapidly fell in love.

Perhaps there was no one at all whom Elizabeth would ever have allowed Lady Catherine to marry, but the Earl of Hertford was in some ways a particularly unpromising candidate, because his family had such a history of political ambition. Not only had his father been the Duke of Somerset, but his uncle, his father's younger brother, had been the Sir Thomas Seymour who had married King Henry VIII's widow Queen Catherine Parr and whose designs on Elizabeth herself had so nearly landed her in trouble when she had been a young and inexperienced girl. Although it seems that both the Earl and Lady Catherine wanted to marry for love and not for political reasons, Elizabeth of course would be most interested in the political implications of the marriage, and on those grounds both the Earl and Lady Catherine knew that she would almost certainly forbid it.

Nevertheless, when Lady Jane had recovered her health and the two girls had returned to court, the Earl and Lady Catherine continued to meet in secret. They tried to enlist the help of Lady Catherine's mother, the Dowager Duchess of Suffolk, but even if the Duchess would have been able to help them she died before she could attempt anything. In desperation, the Earl and Lady Catherine decided to risk everything on a secret marriage, hoping against hope either that some unforeseen circumstance might work in their favour or that Elizabeth could not object too much to a *fait accompli*.

The Maids of Honour were normally supposed to be in constant attendance upon the Queen, but when Elizabeth decided to ride to Eltham for a few days' hunting Lady Catherine seized her opportunity: she tied up one cheek in a handkerchief and claimed that she had such bad toothache that she could not possibly go. Lady Jane was also allowed to stay behind—she was so often ill that there was nothing strange about this. As soon as the Queen's retinue had left, the two girls hurried to the Earl of Hertford's house for the secret wedding. There Lady Jane, to her horror, discovered that her brother in his excitement had forgotten to provide a priest; she had to hurry out and waylay the first one she could find. Then the couple were married, the Earl giving Lady Catherine a ring made up of five circles joined into one and a verse inscribed on it which clearly indicated the Elizabethan love of symbolism:

As circles five by art compact, show but one ring in sight,
So trust uniteth faithful minds, with knot of secret might.
Whose force to break but greedie death no wight possesseth power.
As time and sequel well shall prove, my ring can say no more.

The Earl's bold statement that no one but death could break up their marriage was obviously a brave attempt to convince his new wife that all would be well. Almost immediately, however, things started going wrong. In the first place his sister and Lady Catherine's friend and confidant, Lady Jane, fell ill again, and died. Apart from their grief at her death, it also meant that they had no one to share their secret with. Then the next blow fell when Elizabeth sent the Earl on a mission abroad; and no sooner had he gone than Lady Catherine discovered she was pregnant. Now the Queen would have to know the whole story, but poor Lady Catherine was not brave enough to tell Elizabeth herself.

Instead she chose as her confidant one of the most for-
midable women of the Elizabethan age, Elizabeth Saintlow,
who had been a friend of her mother's and who, after surviving four husbands and living into her eighties, was to go
down to history as Bess of Hardwick, after the name of the
tremendous mansion which she built. It says much for the
anger of Elizabeth that even the indomitable Lady Saintlow,
when Lady Catherine confessed to her her marriage and
pregnancy, did not dare break the news to the queen, and
was indeed furious with Lady Catherine for having made her
a party to this dangerous secret. So Lady Catherine decided
to try another intermediary, and this time she chose the most
powerful person she could think of: Robert Dudley, already
Master of the Horse and later to be Earl of Leicester, who
was both connected with Lady Catherine's own family—his
elder brother Lord Guildford Dudley had been married to
Catherine's unlucky elder sister Lady Jane Grey—and was
also very high indeed in Elizabeth's favour. If Dudley could
not win Elizabeth over, nobody could. The unfortunate
Dudley therefore found himself woken up in the middle of
the night by Lady Catherine in tears at his bedside. Since his
room was next to the Queen's, his first thought was for the
trouble he would get into if Elizabeth should hear her, and
to get rid of Lady Catherine he therefore promised to speak
to the Queen the next morning.

Elizabeth reacted quite as badly as anyone had expected.
Not only was Lady Catherine sent to the Tower—where her
sister Lady Jane Grey had died so young—and the Earl of
Hertford recalled from abroad and sent to the Tower as well,
but even poor Lady Saintlow was briefly imprisoned merely
for having been told what was going on and not having
informed Elizabeth. The Queen's anger was increased when
Lady Catherine, in the Tower, gave birth to a boy, since
this strengthened Lady Catherine's position as a possible
heir to the throne. Worse still, prisoners in the Tower were
allowed considerable freedom to move around within the
Tower confines, taking exercise and visiting each other, and
the Lieutenant of the Tower seems to have taken pity on the
young couple and to have turned a blind eye to their secret
meetings, with the result that not long after the birth of her

first child Lady Catherine became pregnant once more, and produced another son.

There was, however, one thing Elizabeth could do. The Earl of Hertford and Lady Catherine had, after all, married in secret, and it was therefore not easy for them to provide actual proof that the marriage had in fact taken place. Lady Jane Seymour, who had witnessed the wedding, was now dead. The person who would of course have been able to certify that they were indeed legally married would have been the priest who officiated. But now the Earl of Hertford paid the consequences for having forgotten to provide a priest: the one whom Lady Jane had had to go out and find at random proved quite impossible to find again. Elizabeth probably did not seriously believe that a woman of royal blood would compromise her position and her claim to the throne by allowing herself to become pregnant without being legally married; but the evidence was nevertheless good enough to have the marriage declared invalid. Furthermore, there was plague in London, and, however serious Elizabeth thought their offence, she could hardly allow them to stay where they might catch it, so she seized the opportunity to separate husband and wife, sending Lady Catherine to her uncle's house and the Earl to his mother's.

They never saw each other again. Six years later, and still under virtual house arrest, Lady Catherine died at the age of 29, perhaps of the tuberculosis which had earlier killed her cousin King Edward VI. The Earl of Hertford spent various parts of Elizabeth's reign in prison for his repeated attempts to prove that his marriage to Lady Catherine had been legal and that his sons were therefore legitimate. He never succeeded, however. He eventually married twice more.

Two of the Grey sisters had now come to unhappy ends; but there was still one left. Lady Mary Grey was the youngest of the three, and she too served as a Maid of Honour. Like her sister Lady Catherine, Lady Mary did not seem to have much chance of ever being allowed to marry, and in her case it appeared unlikely that she would even find a lover, for she was only four feet tall and a hunchback. But in 1565 the court was stunned to discover that yet another secret marriage had taken place, and this time the most improbable one

78

imaginable: between little Lady Mary Grey, possible heir to the throne of England, and a certain Thomas Keyes, the man who guarded the gate leading from the palace of Whitehall to the landing-stage on the river-bank, who stood at what was for an Elizabethan the absolutely immense height of six feet six inches, and was a widower.

It appeared that Keyes had first of all taken to giving Lady Mary little presents of jewellery and ornaments, and had then told her he loved her and asked her to marry him, and she had agreed. There seems no reason to suppose that, like Lady Catherine's and the Earl of Hertford's, this was not a marriage of genuine affection on both sides; but once again Elizabeth was not interested in the personal so much as in the political aspect of the relationship. Keyes was sent to prison and Lady Mary, as her sister had been, to house arrest in the country; the fact that her husband was a nobody and that she had not committed the additional sin of becoming pregnant probably combined to spare her the Tower. For six years she was shuttled around amongst various keepers, until in 1571 Keyes died, almost immediately after he had at last been let out of prison. Lady Mary pathetically pleaded to be allowed to bring up Keyes's children by his first marriage, but even this consolation was denied her. Now that her husband was dead, though, Lady Mary was granted more freedom, and eventually moved into a household of her own. She did not enjoy it long, though; she died in 1578, aged 34.

Even the punishments meted out to the two Grey girls, however, did not succeed in deterring other people from making secret marriages or, almost as dangerous, having illicit affairs, although everyone at the court knew only too well how great Elizabeth's fury could be when the inevitable discovery was made. When another of the Maids of Honour, Mary Shelton, was discovered to be secretly married to James Scudamore, the Queen physically attacked her and actually broke her finger, but was then so horrified by what she had done that she forgave the couple and allowed the bride to stay on at court. No doubt, on this occasion, she was able to overlook their offence more easily because James Scudamore was not a man in whom she herself felt any great interest.

Her wrath could be even more severe when it was one of her own especial favourites who had been rash enough to make a secret marriage.

It is all too easy to view this aspect of Elizabeth's character as the vanity, jealousy and wounded pride of a foolish, ageing woman who, because she could not enjoy herself, did not want anyone else to do so either. But there is another side to the story. Even Elizabeth's treatment of Lady Catherine and Lady Mary Grey, which may look to us like nothing but wanton cruelty, was, from her point of view, to some extent justified by the need to protect her own position—which in turn would guarantee the political stability of the country—and by the wish to make their punishments act as a deterrent to those who might be tempted to offend similarly. And although Elizabeth would scarcely be human if there were not an element of sour grapes in her attitude to the marriages of her pretty young Maids of Honour to her favourites when she herself was single, childless and losing her looks, yet she could rightly feel aggrieved because a genuine betrayal of her trust had taken place in such cases.

It had long been a feature of European court culture that there were many more eligible young men at court than there were women. This situation might perhaps have given rise to tensions, if the potential danger had not been customarily defused by a court culture in which the status of women was greatly elevated, so that men were encouraged to regard them as a sort of superior being to be worshipped from afar, strictly unattainable, whose rôle was to inspire their knights and encourage them to act nobly. A knight or squire could pick a particular lady as his 'mistress', while he would be her 'servant'; and since the relationship between them was strictly platonic, the same mistress could have many servants, which could provide a safe channel for the emotions of the young men at court. This system could of course very easily break down in practice—the relationship might not remain platonic, or someone, misunderstanding the rules of the game, might become too emotionally involved—but such was the theory, and in modified form it had persisted into the early Tudor courts; it could even be argued that it was a version of this game which had provided the pretext which had enabled Elizabeth's father Henry VIII to execute her mother, Anne Boleyn.

Men vastly outnumbering women was not so much a feature of Elizabeth's court, where a female ruler naturally required an unusual number of female attendants and there was no king with a suite of young men, but the game was still played around Elizabeth herself. The strains and isolation of Elizabeth's position, as well as her unsettled childhood and her lack of any close family, all left her with a great need for emotional warmth and affection; and there was also her vanity and, perhaps, a craving for reassurance of her identity as a woman, since the function of ruler which she fulfilled was traditionally so much a male one; indeed it is common in the period to find Elizabeth referred to, or referring to herself, as a prince or a king rather than a queen.

All this led her to want to surround herself with young, handsome and adoring men; and such young men, in turn, were usually happy to provide romantic devotion in return for the favour of the Queen, a secure position at court, and the more tangible benefits like land, money and office which almost always followed. Some of them, indeed, seem genuinely to have felt the devotion they professed: Sir Christopher Hatton never married for the Queen's sake, and very few of her favourites could have been indifferent to the charisma and magnetism she still possessed even after her looks had deserted her. As the reign progressed, however, the terms in which the courtiers proclaimed their feelings for the Virgin Queen became so extravagant that perhaps nobody could really have believed in them; and many of the Queen's courtiers also had lands and positions to think of. It was an age when family and descent counted for a great deal, when people died young and unexpectedly, and when it was a commonplace that the only way to outwit death was to secure immortality by having children—an idea which can be seen at work, for instance, in Shakespeare's sonnets. Many of Elizabeth's courtiers were not prepared to risk the extinction of their families by staying single, while others were simply in love, or, as in the case, late in the reign, of the Earl of Essex, acted from a sense of obligation. Their motives, however, were of little or no interest to Elizabeth: she simply regarded every such marriage as a betrayal of the devotion which they had so often sworn to her. The court culture of Elizabethan England might be glittering and splendid, but it held dangers too.

V

The Court System Tested: The Earl of Essex

BOTH the rewards and the dangers of court life are graphically illustrated by the career of Robert Devereux, Earl of Essex. Essex was given his start at court by his stepfather, Robert Dudley, Earl of Leicester, one of the earliest and most important of all the Queen's favourites. Contemporaries thought Elizabeth would have married Leicester had it not been for the mysterious death of his wife, and she scandalized watchers when she tickled his neck in public. She sent him to the Netherlands as the leader of her armies there, and for him she even relaxed her customary carefulness with money, giving him Kenilworth Castle and also making him loans. But even Leicester's position was not impregnable. He felt the lash of her tongue when he rashly contemplated accepting the offer of the Netherlanders to make him their king. He also had a close escape when the widowed Lady Sheffield claimed that he had secretly married her and was the father of the child she was now expecting; but although Leicester acknowledged the child, he denied the marriage vehemently and, as so often with secret marriages, Lady Sheffield was unable to produce sufficient evidence to prove that it had taken place, if indeed it had.

If there had indeed been a secret marriage with Lady Sheffield, it is interesting that Leicester denied it, because acknowledging it would have brought him not only a wife, but also an heir, since Lady Sheffield gave birth to a son. Leicester's property, when he died, would go to his nephew Sir Philip Sidney, the son of his sister Mary; but fond though Leicester was of Sir Philip, either his desire for an heir or genuine love soon got him entangled again. This time the woman in question was Lettice Knollys (the name is a shortened form of Laetitia, the Latin for happiness).

Lettice's father, Sir Francis Knollys, was the son of Catherine Carey, whose mother Mary Boleyn had been the sister of Queen Anne Boleyn; Lettice was therefore a cousin of Queen Elizabeth, and, so far as can be judged from surviving portraits, she also looked rather like her. She also seems to have shared some of her royal cousin's determination and strength of mind. She had been married to Walter Devereux, Earl of Essex, and they had had four children, but then Elizabeth had sent the Earl to that graveyard of so many Elizabethan careers, Ireland, where her unfortunate officials were supposed to maintain order against a hostile native population with insufficient money, insufficient troops and irregularly received orders. The strain had told on the Earl's health and, after spending considerable amounts of his money on the Queen's service, he had fallen sick and died.

The Earl of Leicester was already unpopular, and rumours soon spread that he had poisoned the Earl of Essex in order to be able to marry his widow. Although this story is extremely unlikely to be true, Leicester and Lettice did, indeed, marry secretly; but in order that Lettice would not find herself in the same position as Lady Sheffield had done, her father, Sir Francis Knollys, insisted on another ceremony, which he attended himself. This second wedding was also secret, for Leicester's position at court would be completely undermined if Elizabeth discovered that he was married, but court gossip travelled fast and there were plenty of people at court who either envied Leicester's standing with Elizabeth or felt that he was a bad influence on her, and so were prepared to reveal his secret. It was the time of the Duke of Alençon's visit to England, and Leicester, fearing that his own power would diminish if the Queen had a husband, had been doing everything he could to prevent the marriage. It was, therefore, a godsend for Alençon's chief adviser when he discovered this piece of news which could be used with such devastating effect to discredit Leicester, and he lost no time in telling the Queen.

The Queen's rage was so great that at first she wanted to send Leicester to the Tower. She was only dissuaded by the Earl of Sussex, one of her most reliable counsellors, who was in fact a sworn enemy of Leicester's but who did not think that, where there were no political considerations, it was reasonable to imprison a man for getting married, and who did not want to see the Queen make herself ridiculous by acting out of jealousy and spite. Instead Elizabeth was persuaded to send Leicester away from court and to let it be known that the reason for his absence was a sudden illness.

Soon, however, Leicester's long hold on Elizabeth's affections began to reassert itself, and he was allowed back into her presence; he was treated coldly, but he had at least been given the opportunity to try to make himself agreeable enough to re-establish himself in her good graces. The person Elizabeth could not forgive, however, was her cousin Lettice Knollys. She would refer to her only as 'that she-wolf', and refused absolutely to allow her to come to court. She even made Sussex look into the old story that Leicester had been secretly married to Lady Sheffield, apparently thinking that that if Leicester had to be married at all then at least it need not be to Lettice. Lady Sheffield, however, was in an awkward position, because when Leicester's marriage to Lettice became known and she realized that she no longer had any hope of persuading him to acknowledge her as his wife, she had married somebody else. If she still maintained that she had in fact been married to Leicester, her new marriage would be bigamous; so under the circumstances she seems to have felt it best to cut her losses and hang on to the husband she had rather than keep trying to secure the elusive Leicester.

The Queen therefore had to be informed that there was no hope from that quarter, and that Leicester's marriage to Lettice would have to be recognized. Soon it looked even more solid when a son, called Robert like his father, was born to the new Countess of Leicester. Ironically, however, this child was later to die young, while Leicester's son by Lady Sheffield, also called Robert, lived to adulthood and married, but, because his father had not acknowledged his legitimacy, was never able to claim the Leicester inheritance. If it was indeed the survival of his family which Leicester was trying to ensure by his marriage, he was to be unsuccessful.

The death of their son, however, must have been less of a blow to Lettice than to Leicester, for she already had four children from her first marriage (the eldest, Penelope, was to become the 'Stella' of Sir Philip Sidney's sequence of sonnets 'Astrophil and Stella'). When Lettice married Leicester the elder of her two sons, Robert Devereux, was 13 and, since the death of his father, was already Earl of Essex. Leicester took an interest in his stepson, and took him to court to present him to the Queen, who was much taken with the handsome boy and disappointed that, in typical adolescent fashion, he would not let her kiss him. The young Earl was sent to Cambridge, but then disappointed his ambitious relatives by going to live quietly and privately on his ancestral estates in South Wales rather than going to court. Eventually they managed to persuade him that this was no place for a young and handsome nobleman, and that his duty to his family required him to go to court.

There were various reasons why his relatives should want him to do this. Although Essex was an earl, he was not rich: his father's campaigns in Ireland, on which he had spent his own money when there was none forthcoming from the Queen, had left the family fortunes in a poor state. To compensate for this deficiency, Essex could either resign himself to living quietly, as he had been doing, or he could gamble by going to the court, where to maintain a suitable standard of living would cost much more but where he might, perhaps, gain the Queen's favour and consequently be able to rebuild his shattered finances. If he succeeded in this, the rewards could be expected to fall not only to him but also to his whole family, who were still in disgrace after his mother Lettice's marriage to Leicester.

He could also help Leicester, his stepfather, who was greying and ageing now and felt that he was having difficulty maintaining his position as favourite in the face of competition from the many younger and more dashing men now at court. Leicester felt that the time had come for him to 'retire' from the position of favourite, but he wanted to make sure that the rewards that the position brought continued to go to his family. What better way than to introduce his stepson, just 21 and with striking looks and a temperament that was a mixture of passion, pride and charm, to the Queen and hope that he caught her fancy?

So there began the most extraordinary and most passionate of Elizabeth's relationships with her favourites. She was 54 when Essex came to court, old enough to be his mother and perhaps, given the young age of marriage in the period, even his grandmother; but although she had lost her looks she had kept her figure, her energy, her wit and, perhaps most important of all, her vanity, which made it very easy for her to overlook the differences between them and to see the relationship in the traditional terms of beautiful, inaccessible mistress and humble, adoring servant.

Furthermore, the cult of the Virgin Queen was by now so well-established at court and, to a lesser extent, in the country as a whole, that her subjects had in some sense ceased to regard her as a woman at all: she had taken on almost the proportions of a goddess, a mythological figure, or a symbol of the greatness of the age. It does not do justice to Elizabeth to regard her relationship with Essex as the doting passion of an ageing woman for a pretty but petulant boy; it was equally, and perhaps more so, a manifestation of the power of her personality and of the mystique which she had woven around herself, and although Essex was frequently infuriated by her, he does also seem to have been genuinely fascinated by her. What one can deduce of his character does not make him appear the sort of sycophant who would have kept up the pretence of a passion for a woman unless there had been some sort of grain of truth, an element of genuine interest or respect, to their relationship. If that had been his nature, matters would probably not have ended as they did.

For although the relationship between Elizabeth and Essex lasted for fourteen years, it was very often a stormy one. Essex was not like his stepfather Leicester; indeed he was not like any of Elizabeth's favourites, who were usually careful to flatter her, compliment her and at least appear to be doing what she wanted. Although Essex might do all these things occasionally, he was equally capable of reproaching her, disobeying her and flinging off from court in high dudgeon, leaving Elizabeth to send after him or to mollify him. This was not the rôle the Queen was used to playing, and she did not particularly like it. Sometimes she too would refuse to give in; but her position was weaker, because her vanity, her loneliness and her craving for an emotional outlet meant that her need for Essex was far greater than his for her.

Indeed Essex's relationship to Elizabeth is in some ways reminiscent of that of Elizabeth's own mother, Anne Boleyn, to that of her father King Henry VIII. Anne Boleyn, daughter of an ambitious father, had been sent to court so that she might in some way bring benefits to her family, but she had, unexpectedly, hooked a bigger fish than she was angling for when Henry VIII fell in love with her. And what was she to do? If she refused him, her family would certainly be disgraced. The logic of the court, where courtiers competed for the prizes offered by court life, dictated that Anne must accept the King whatever her own feelings might be on the matter. Similarly Essex, having once come to court, had to live by the rules of the court for as long as Elizabeth wanted him there.

And Elizabeth showed no signs of being willing to let him go. Indeed her need of him increased, for in September 1588, two months after the defeat of the Spanish Armada, Essex's stepfather the Earl of Leicester, travelling on his usual journey to the famous spa waters of Buxton, fell ill and died, probably of malaria. When Elizabeth was told she locked herself into her room for two days, seeing no one, eating nothing, until her faithful minister William Cecil, Lord Burghley, took the risk that perhaps no one else would have dared take and had her door broken down. Elizabeth came out, but the blow had been a hard one to her; just how hard was shown after her death when the little box of private treasures that she kept by her bedside was opened and was found to contain the last note she had ever received from Leicester, carefully folded up and labelled in her own handwriting 'His last letter'. The death of Leicester had not only robbed her of the man to whom she had been close for thirty years, it was also the first serious reminder of her own mortality, and of how lonely her remaining years might be once her old friends started dying. Now more than ever she needed youth about her, and Essex in particular, for his own sake, and also, perhaps, because he was Leicester's stepson.

Essex, however, had other ideas. It might be traditional for young noblemen to come to court and display their powers of dancing, conversation, music-making and so forth, but, until very recently, the primary rôle of the nobility had been to seek military glory, and, however much Elizabeth might dislike war, many of the young men at her court thirsted for what they saw as a chance to prove their worth in action. They were influenced not so much by the reality of fighting—which, thanks to the peace maintained so carefully by Elizabeth, few of them had ever seen—as by glamorous images of it: the prowess of the Arthurian knights whom they encountered so often in their reading and in court entertainments; the glorious combats of Homer which the new feeling for classical literature made more widely studied; and, above all, by the cult of mediaeval chivalry which formed so important a part of Elizabethan tournaments but was a far cry from the bogs of Ireland, the muddy fields of the Netherlands and the realities of sixteenth-century warfare, which was more likely to feature clumsy guns and cannon than the shining swords and spears of the tales and romances. Sir Philip Sidney had ridden out like a knight of old to take on the forces of Spain, but he had been unceremoniously felled by a musket ball in his thigh and died of gangrene. Elizabeth thought that her impetuous young courtiers should learn their lesson from Sidney's death, but they did not. Some went so far as to run away to fight; others pleaded with her so much that eventually her resolve was worn down and she gave in. Sir Walter Raleigh went to America, and Essex to Cadiz and the Azores and, following his father, to Ireland.

His military career, however, was a chequered one. He had some success in Cadiz, though that was a little marred by his feuding with Sir Walter Raleigh and Lord Howard of Effingham, the Lord Admiral, about who should take the credit for the expedition; but the voyage to the Azores was a fiasco. It was again the scene of rivalry and bickering between Essex and Raleigh, and it failed utterly to produce any of the looted Spanish treasure that, to Elizabeth, was the only possible justification for such a costly and dangerous expedition. Although she cried with joy when she heard that he was safe, she was nevertheless very angry at his expensive failure, and she told Lord Burghley that this was the last time she would ever allow her fleet to go further than the English Channel. It did not make Elizabeth any happier that many people in the court and amongst the public at large were prepared to put the failure of the voyage down to sheer bad luck and to regard Essex as a new military hero. His stepfather Leicester had never been popular; but Essex was. And Elizabeth found that she did not altogether relish his popularity. Like so many unmilitary rulers with successful generals, she felt that Essex's popularity in some way impinged on the devotion which should be due solely to her, and perhaps partly because of this she decided to bestow an unusual honour on Lord Howard of Effingham, the man who had shared responsibility for the Cadiz expedition with Essex. Elizabeth was normally very reluctant to bestow honours and peerages, but now she created Lord Howard Earl of Nottingham.

This new title, together with his existing rank as Lord Admiral, meant that the new Earl of Nottingham would take precedence over all other earls, including Essex. To take precedence meant walking first in state processions, sitting nearest to the head of the table, passing first through doors: all things which may seem now to be so trivial that it would be ludicrous to worry about them, but which were accepted in the Elizabethan age as clear indications of a person's status and power. Essex had already had disputes over precedence with Lord Howard of Effingham before his elevation to the earldom, and now, rather than come to court and have to give way publicly to his rival, he stayed at home. He announced that he was sick and could not come to court.

This was potentially a dangerous situation. The aim of the elaborate Elizabethan court culture was precisely to prevent great nobles from retreating to the country, where they could build up private followings and personal popularity without the Queen being able to keep a watchful eye on them; for a great lord like Essex to feel able to stay away from court challenged the whole basis of the courtly mythology that

Elizabeth was like a sun and that her adoring courtiers would waste away without the daily sight of her. The situation was particularly serious because it was coming up to the time of the annual tilt held to celebrate the day on which Elizabeth had come to the throne, and for Essex to stay away from that would both spoil Elizabeth's pleasure in the day and also raise in people's minds the daring and dangerous suggestion that there might be life beyond the court.

Stay away he did, however. The Queen's cousin, Lord Hunsdon, wrote to him suggesting his return; even the new Earl of Nottingham sent him a conciliatory letter—to which Essex's only reply was a typically chivalric offer of single combat, prudently refused by Nottingham, who was many years older than Essex. Eventually Essex let it be known that he would return to court if the Queen specifically asked him to, but Elizabeth was not prepared to compromise her dignity by having to plead with a petulant subject. The situation was becoming electric. When the French ambassador suggested to Elizabeth that Essex had not done his duty to her on his voyage to the Azores, she replied that if that had really been the case she would have cut off his head, and no one could be sure whether this was a joke or not.

Nobody knew how the situation eventually came to be resolved, but it seems likely that somehow a compromise between the stubborn Earl and the no less stubborn Queen was secretly negotiated. After a two-month absence, the Earl unexpectedly reappeared at court, and the Queen immediately conferred on him the office of Earl Marshal of England. This post, which involved the arrangement of tournaments and the superintending of the heralds and the courts of chivalry, was ideally suited to Essex's chivalric interests, and it also gave him precedence over the Earl of Nottingham, thus enabling him to maintain his dignity and not have to give in to his rival. It was also, perhaps rather ominously, a job which had been left vacant by the Queen's execution, earlier in the reign, of her cousin the Earl of Norfolk for plotting to marry Mary, Queen of Scots; but Essex seemed to feel no unease about thus stepping into a dead man's shoes, and his position at court appeared to be as secure as ever. He

even appeared to have succeeded in the seemingly impossible task of persuading the Queen to forgive his mother, her
old enemy Lettice Knollys, and to receive her at court for the
first time since her secret marriage to the Earl of Leicester had
been disclosed.

The only cloud remaining on the horizon appeared to
be the Earl's propensity to flirt with the Maids of Honour:
Elizabeth's godson, Sir John Harington, reported a terrible
scene when one of them, Lady Mary Howard, appeared
in an immensely rich velvet dress decorated with pearls,
which clearly caught Essex's eye. As soon as Elizabeth was
back in her own apartments she sent for the dress and put
it on, although Lady Mary was far shorter than she and the
dress consequently came only half-way down her legs and
arms. She then appalled the Maids of Honour by appearing
before them dressed like this and asking them how they
liked her 'new-fancied suit', before addressing Lady Mary
directly and asking her if she did not think that the dress
was too short and did not suit her. Lady Mary could only
agree, whereupon Elizabeth told her that if the dress was too
short for a queen it was certainly too elaborate for a Maid of
Honour, and departed. That was the last Lady Mary saw of
her dress. Elizabeth's jealousy of her favourites was as strong
as ever, but at least this time she could take what comfort she
could from the fact that Essex at least could not have secretly
married Lady Mary, even if he had wanted to, for the simple
reason that shortly before this episode he had confessed that
he was already secretly married.

Essex's marriage, unlike that of his stepfather Leicester
to his mother Lettice Knollys, was, however, no matter of
overriding passion. Like so many things in Essex's life, it
was dictated by motives of chivalry. The great friend of
his youth had been Sir Philip Sidney, who had been in
love with Essex's sister Penelope and to whom Essex, like
so many others, had looked up as the pattern of English
knighthood. Sir Philip had thought equally highly of Essex
and, as he lay dying of gangrene, he had bequeathed to
Essex his best sword—symbol of his knighthood—and his
wife, Frances Walsingham. Frances was the daughter of Sir
Francis Walsingham, an ardent Protestant who had been

the organizer of Elizabeth's secret service but who was now old, sick and heavily in debt. He would be unable to do very much for his daughter, who was pregnant, and it was Sidney's concern for what might happen to his family after his death that led him to ask Essex to make the best possible provision for Frances by marrying her, thus making her Countess of Essex and giving her and her unborn child a secure home and future.

Essex had fulfilled his friend's request, but, knowing what Elizabeth's reaction was likely to be, had kept the marriage secret. But it does not seem to have been in his nature to conceal things, and when Frances became pregnant he lost no time in personally informing the queen of what he had done. Elizabeth, as expected, was annoyed, objecting particularly to the fact that Frances's relatively low birth made her an unsuitable wife for an earl. But perhaps because Essex had at least had the courage to tell her himself, or perhaps because she had simply got tired of berating people about their marriages, she took the news relatively calmly. Although it was understood that the new Countess would not be welcome at court, her displeasure with Essex was over within the unusually short time of a fortnight.

Much more serious was the affair of his expedition to Ireland. Ireland had been a headache for Elizabeth throughout her reign, and it was even more so for the generals whom she sent there, who had not only to contend with the damp climate, the lack of the amenities to which they were accustomed at home, and the desperation of a determined and resourceful people fighting for their land, but were also very rarely given enough money, were cut off from the court, the seat of power, and were expected to act on Elizabeth's instructions, although the delay involved in getting news from Ireland to the court and orders back there again almost invariably meant that the instructions they were sent bore no relation to the situation as it had since developed. The Irish problem seemed insoluble, but Elizabeth and her ministers knew that they had to go on making attempts to solve it, because Ireland represented the back door to England, and its Catholicism made it an attractive landing-point for enemy forces from Catholic Europe, as had already been demonstrated by the Spanish. It was also galling to the Queen that her image as an adored ruler was tarnished by the fact that her supposed subjects in Ireland so obviously did not adore her. She wanted the question of Ireland dealt with for good and all, and called a meeting of her Council to deal with the question of who was the best person to do it.

The meeting was to be a momentous one. For some time now there had had been tension at court between the Earl of Essex and the only two men whose influence with the Queen almost rivalled his own, her most trusted counsellor, the old Lord Treasurer William Cecil (now Lord Burghley) and the Treasurer's brilliant, hunchbacked son, Robert Cecil, who looked set to succeed his father as the Queen's chief minister. After the death of Essex's father, Burghley had been his guardian, and had taken good care of his interests, but now Essex was opposed to the Treasurer and his son on almost every count. Old Lord Burghley, who in his youth had followed the English army on its ravaging of Scotland, shared the Queen's intense dislike for the cost and waste of war; so, whenever Essex urged a military expedition in search of wealth and glory, the Cecils argued against him. Their policy was caution, whereas his was always full of youthful impetuosity. And the Queen, with her loathing of committing herself and of decisive actions, was, too often for Essex's liking, inclined to listen to the Cecils rather than to him. He might be her undisputed favourite, Earl Marshal of England, a military hero and a far finer figure in the tiltyard than poor deformed Robert Cecil could ever be, but he was nevertheless finding that when important jobs became vacant Elizabeth was just as likely to give them to friends of the Cecils as she was to friends of his. This diminished Essex's importance in the public eye and meant that fewer people were likely to support him. He began to regard the Cecils as dangerous enemies.

It was against this background that the meeting took place to decide who was to be sent to Ireland. For once in her life, the Queen had actually come to a decision, and now she put it forward for the approval of her counsellors: she felt that Sir William Knollys, whose sister Lettice was Essex's mother, was the best person to go. Perhaps she thought that Essex would be pleased to see his uncle given the job, but if so she was mistaken. Instead he regarded it as a serious threat: if his uncle was sent to Ireland, he would have one fewer supporter at court. He would far rather see the Cecils robbed of a friend instead, and so he proposed Sir George Carew, whom he knew to be a supporter of theirs whom they might find it hard to manage without. Elizabeth, however, having finally made a decision, proposed to stick to it, and said no.

But Essex would not take no for an answer. He repeated his request, which was beginning to sound dangerously like a demand; the Queen persisted in her refusal. It was turning into an embarrassing public scene. Finally, the Queen told Essex that whatever he might say, his uncle was being sent to Ireland, and that was that. In complete defiance of all court etiquette, Essex insultingly turned his back on her. However fond she might be of her favourite, Elizabeth could not stand for that: she marched up behind him and boxed him soundly on the ears, shouting 'Go to the devil!' And Essex, wheeling round, yelling back at her that he would not have tolerated such an outrage from her father himself, reached for his sword.

To draw a blade even in the presence of the sovereign was an offence; to threaten her with one was high treason. Essex's old adversary the Earl of Nottingham immediately leaped between his Queen and the Earl, pushing Essex backwards. Elizabeth, a brave woman, stood motionless. Essex's hand fell away from his sword and, turning, he ran from the room.

He went straight to the country. Since what he had done was monstrous, unthinkable and without precedent, people had no idea what would happen next; if the Queen so wished, she would certainly be well within the law in imposing almost any penalty she chose, even death. But the Queen did not wish. Whatever he had done to her, Essex was still too dear to her to be punished. But nor could such behaviour be overlooked. He had insulted and threatened her in front of her counsellors, and before he could be forgiven and trusted again there had to be a proper apology and some signs of real repentance. Although he did write

to her from his country retreat, the letter contained no word
of apology and concentrated instead on his own offended
dignity. Elizabeth retorted that 'he hath played long enough
upon me and now I mean to play awhile with him and stand
as much upon my greatness as he hath upon his stomach'
(stomach being an Elizabethan term for pride). She would let
him sit and stew in the country until he was ready to treat
her properly.

Meanwhile she had other things to worry her. The
first blow fell when it became clear that her much-trusted
treasurer Lord Burghley, her closest adviser since the very
beginning of her reign, was dying. This was the greatest
calamity Elizabeth had suffered since the death of Leicester,
and in many ways it was more serious. It robbed her of the
man she trusted most, who knew how to deal with her
moods and who also had an obvious deep affection for her;
and it underlined the increasing loneliness she faced in her
old age as, one by one, her old friends died around her. The
problem of Essex was left on one side now as she spent her
time at Burghley's bedside, feeding him with her own hand
in a vain attempt to prolong his life. When he died she wept
as she had not wept since the loss of Leicester, and could
never hear his name without shedding tears.

Burghley's death was followed with cruel suddenness
by another disaster: bad news from Ireland. A large English
army had been utterly crushed and its leader killed, by the
Earl of Tyrone, the leader of the native Irish forces. It was
England's worst military defeat for years and her whole
position in Ireland appeared to be completely undermined.
Elizabeth needed a miracle, or at the very least an exception-
ally able general; and, still isolated in his country retreat,
Essex, hearing the terrible news, decided that he was the
man she needed.

Perhaps he saw this as a chance to repair the breach and
recover his position as favourite; perhaps he was attracted
as usual by the prospect of military glory; perhaps he was
moved by patriotism or a genuine affection for Elizabeth and
a belief that he could help her: whatever his motives, he
went at once to Whitehall to make his offer. Elizabeth, however, would not even see him, instructing a messenger to

'tell the Earl that I value *myself* at as great a price as he values *himself*.' Essex tried a softer, more tactful line of approach: he informed the Queen that 'as a man, I have been more subject to your natural beauty than as a subject to the power of a king.' Elizabeth was sufficiently mollified by this flattery to agree to see him, but she still wanted to be regarded both as a woman and as a Queen as well, and when no apology was forthcoming for the insult to her royal dignity, she refused to give him the appointment. Once again, Essex absented himself from court and returned to the country.

To have great nobles skulking in the country in times of national crisis was exactly what the Elizabethan court system was designed to avoid. Elizabeth had devoted great energy to projecting an image of herself as an all-powerful, all-adored monarch of quasi-divine status; Essex's attitude blemished that image and harked back most disturbingly to the attitudes of the great magnates of the pre-Tudor period, who had tended to regard the King not as a being mystically set apart from them but rather as one of their own number to whom they had agreed in a sort of mutual contract to give authority, but from whom they could equally well take it away if they did not like the way he used it. Indeed, a letter written by Essex to one of his friends at court shows his thinking as being very much in the cast of mind of a great mediaeval aristocrat: 'What, cannot princes err? Cannot subjects receive wrong? Is an earthly power or authority infinite? Pardon me, pardon me, my good Lord, I can never subscribe to these principles.' Elizabeth would have known better than openly to ask him to subscribe to any such principles, but nevertheless it was inherent and implicit in the image she had created for herself that princes could *not* err and that an earthly power or authority *could* be infinite. Essex's way of thinking would have seemed to her to be a dangerous throwback to the sort of aristocrats who had launched the rebellions against the crown of her father's and sister's reigns, but which, partly by her creation of a powerful personal cult, she seemed to have eliminated so successfully from her own.

But if Elizabeth enjoyed great personal popularity in the country, so too did Essex. He was handsome, generous, polite, and had a reputation for military prowess and also, although in fact he had many Catholic friends, for staunch Protestantism (he was felt to have inherited the position of Sir Philip Sidney in the forefront of European Protestant chivalry, and the firmly Protestant University of Cambridge invited him to succeed Lord Burghley in the post of its Chancellor). Elizabeth, keenly observant of public opinion, was aware of Essex's popularity, and that some people might even go so far as to think that it was she, and not he, who was to blame for their estrangement. Perhaps she began to feel that it might actually be safer to have Essex out of the way in Ireland; perhaps she was tired of the quarrel and wanted to be on good terms again. When news came that the Earl had become ill, Elizabeth saw an opportunity for reconciliation, and took it: she sent her own doctor to him and let it be known that she had decided to forgive him. She had already sent a new commander, Sir Richard Bingham, to Ireland, but Bingham had scarcely arrived when he took ill and died. Now Elizabeth finally agreed to send Essex instead.

Before he set off, though, there was another upset—nothing serious for Essex in itself, but to the superstitious Elizabethan mind, something that could be interpreted as a bad omen for him. A book was published on the reign of King Henry IV, who had been king of England from 1399 to 1413, and whose reign was a very sensitive topic in English history because he had acquired the throne by deposing and killing his cousin, King Richard II. Just as in the twentieth century it is argued that seeing events portrayed on television, film or video can influence some people to mimic what they have seen, so in the sixteenth century it was believed that recounting or enacting events could stimulate people to perform similar things. It was forbidden to depict riots of apprentices in plays in case it encouraged the real apprentices, present in the audience, to riot; and similarly, when a play (probably the one by Shakespeare) was put on about the reign of Richard II, Elizabeth's officials insisted on the removal of the scene which showed Richard being deposed, in case it planted in people's minds the thoroughly undesirable idea that it might be possible for their own

Queen to be deposed. The book that now came out, written by a man named John Hayward, also contained a long account of Richard's deposition, to which Elizabeth objected violently: she said to the Keeper of the Tower when he asked her why she felt so strongly about the Richard II question, 'I am Richard II, know ye not that?', meaning that she felt that any account of Richard's deposition was bound to have a contemporary political reference.

The book's subject matter, then, was already offensive to the queen. But there was an added complication. John Hayward, like many writers of the time, had chosen to introduce his book with a message of dedication to a powerful figure whose prestige might enhance that of the work itself—and the dedicatee he had chosen was Essex. It might have been pure chance that he did so; but it just so happened that the man who had deposed Richard II, and had gone on to become King Henry IV, had previously had the title of Earl of Hereford, and one of Essex's other titles, as Hayward pointed out in the dedication, was Viscount Hereford. One interpretation of the book and the dedication could be that Elizabeth was being compared with Richard II and Essex himself with Henry IV, and that Essex was in fact being covertly invited to depose Elizabeth.

As soon as the Queen became aware of the book she summoned Francis Bacon, who was one of her legal advisers, and asked him whether or not Hayward could be prosecuted for treason. Bacon, who was a friend of Essex, attempted to turn the matter into a joke by saying that he did not think there was enough evidence to support a charge of treason but that Hayward could certainly be prosecuted for theft because he had stolen so many passages in his book from the Roman historian Tacitus. Hayward, however, was sent to the Tower. The question of whether or not Essex had been involved, and if so what in, was allowed to blow over, because the Earl was so busily preparing to emulate not Henry IV but his own father, the previous Earl of Essex, who had also been commander in Ireland. Finally, in March 1599, the Earl set sail.

Francis Bacon, the Earl's friend, had, some time earlier, advised him that if he *pretended* he wanted to go to Ireland,

99

the native Irish would be so frightened when they heard he was coming that they would immediately surrender, and Essex would then get all the glory without having had to do any work. That, however, was not Essex's way. He seems to have been too direct, too passionate, too sure of his own rightness and too conscious of his own honour to have been able to deceive; he had said he would go to Ireland, so he would go. He seems, though, to have become gradually aware that in fact the plan had many disadvantages. Originally he had thought his interests might suffer without his uncle in England to help him look after them; now he began to realize that they were likely to suffer much more without himself there to see to them. Robert Cecil would have the ear of the Queen all to himself; he would not be able to exercise his greatest weapon, the effect on Elizabeth of his personal magnetism; and Ireland, which had defeated Essex's father and brought him to an early grave, might yet prove too much for Essex himself. He was, however, far too proud to turn back. And there would be some consolations: if he was cut off from Elizabeth and the court, it meant, by the same token, that they could not interfere too closely with him. For the first time since he had entered public life, he would have, in effect, a completely free hand.

Elizabeth, who was only too well aware that she could not exercise such close supervision as she would have liked on her deputies in Ireland, had laid down strict instructions for Essex to follow. In particular she was concerned about the people he proposed to appoint to office. Essex's major grievance against the Cecil family had been that they got for their friends jobs which he had wanted to go to his own friends; now that he was in command of an army Elizabeth obviously suspected that he was going to be more open-handed than she liked in giving appointments and honours to his followers. Before he left England she had already vetoed two appointments he had made: she removed his mother's third husband, a Catholic, from his council, and Essex's best friend, the Earl of Southampton, from the position of General of the Horse—Southampton had recently committed the classic courtier's crime of secretly marrying a Maid of Honour whom he had made pregnant, and the Queen had not forgiven him for it. She also instructed Essex that he was to give knighthoods only to men who had shown exceptional valour in battle, and that he was to march against the Earl of Tyrone in his Ulster stronghold as soon as he landed.

These orders Essex disobeyed. Possibly he felt that an elderly, war-hating queen, safely tucked away in England, could not possibly know as much as he did about what was the right way to conquer and subdue a country; at all events, he was soon lavishly distributing knighthoods among his captains, in direct defiance of Elizabeth's orders and despite her known dislike of over-liberal distribution of honours, and he also decided not to obey her commands and march on Tyrone. Instead he squandered time, money and men on bringing to submission some of the less important towns and castles. His argument was that it would be easier to deal with Tyrone once he was in control of the rest of the country, but he soon realized that his army was now too small for him to have any real hope against Tyrone.

Things were rapidly beginning to look very black for Essex. He found the Irish climate uncongenial and fell ill, as his father had done before him; he became convinced that Robert Cecil and his friends had succeeded in poisoning the Queen's mind against him; he felt betrayed by his soldiers, and even went so far as to imprison all the officers of one particular detachment which he felt had betrayed him by behaving in a cowardly manner, and kill every tenth soldier from it—which of course depleted his troops still further. In the end he was forced to write to the Queen confessing that he had lost three-quarters of his army: of the 16,000 men he had brought only 4,000 remained, and he urgently needed more. Elizabeth could spare him only 2,000, and with them she sent a sharp letter reprimanding him for wasting his time, for having created fifty-nine new knights, and for not having marched on Tyrone yet. He was not to come home, she told him, till he had done so.

Elizabeth found her favourite's behaviour very disappointing. She also began to find it worrying. She asked Francis Bacon, once a friend of Essex but now trying to dissociate himself from the Earl's sinking fortunes, what he made of the situation in Ireland, and he gave her an answer which Elizabeth, stateswoman as she was, must surely have thought of for herself but had been unwilling to consider: that perhaps she had not been wise to put Essex at the head of an army. Bacon put it with terrifying clarity: 'to discontent him as you do, and yet to put arms and power into his hands, may be a kind of temptation to him to prove cumbersome and unruly.' He was warning Elizabeth that she might find herself facing a rebellion.

Bacon's words were prophetic. Back in Ireland, the thoughts of Essex and his friends had already begun to wander in the same direction. For centuries past the ancestors of Essex and of people like him had turned to rebellion when they felt the sovereign was acting improperly; to Elizabeth, such an action might seem simple treason, but there was a strong aristocratic tradition which interpreted it quite differently, as the nobility exercising its duty to ensure good government. Usually, of course, action had been taken by some or all of the nobility had banded together, rather than just one, but Essex already had his friend the Earl of Southampton on his side, and he seems to have been confident that many more people would flock to join him once they knew what he was doing. It would be a conflict of ideas about government—the old aristocracy-centred one of Essex, or the king-centred one which Elizabeth and her Tudor ancestors had been trying so hard to impose in its place—and Essex, to judge from his behaviour, was sure that his view would prevail. He could even convince himself that his action was perfectly justified: if, as he believed, the Cecil party was plotting his downfall at home, it was only self-protection to forestall them by plotting a rebellion which would topple them from power for ever and would ensure that the Queen would listen to his own, better, advice. Essex's intention seems to have been not to harm the Queen at all, but to make sure that she remained only as the figurehead of a government of which he himself was the real ruler.

It was easier to talk about than to do, however. Essex had family connections and considerable personal support in south Wales, and thought at first of trying to imitate Elizabeth's own grandfather Henry Tudor by landing there and marching to London, hoping to gather support as he went. It was his stepfather who showed him that this would mean war, whereas it would be much simpler to go to London, muster a much smaller force there and take control of the government, ousting Essex's enemy Robert Cecil, to whom the Queen had just given the profitable post of Master of the Wards, which Essex had wanted for himself.

But even this second plan was still a momentous step, and one that Essex would prefer not to take unless he felt it to be absolutely necessary. He decided first to make one last attempt at regaining Elizabeth's favour by marching against Tyrone.

From the first, the campaign went badly. A force that Essex sent out as a diversionary tactic was massacred, and even when he finally tracked down the enemy army, Tyrone refused to fight. Instead he offered peace talks, and terms—a six-week renewable truce. Essex's situation must have seemed almost desperate; for all his proud offers, he had shown himself unable to resolve the Irish problem. Perhaps he thought that a truce with Tyrone would mean that he had at least not been defeated, or perhaps his increasingly desperate situation had numbed his brain past thinking. He agreed to the proposed truce.

He knew that Elizabeth would be furious, but he seems to have felt that if he could only talk to her, he could justify his decision to her. He ignored the fact that her last letter had told him not to come home until he had subdued Tyrone; he sailed at once and went straight to London. Elizabeth and her court were at the palace of Nonsuch, in Surrey, so to cross the Thames and reach them Essex left behind most of his party and was rowed across with only six of his friends. The only horses they could find were already tired, and so they were overtaken on the way by someone they knew to be a friend of Robert Cecil. One of Essex's followers wanted to kill him, so that he would be unable to warn Cecil of their imminent arrival, but Essex decided against it. Instead they pressed on to the Court, and once arrived, Essex leaped straight from his horse and, still covered in mud from his ride and travel stains from his long journey, he ran up the stairs and burst straight into the Queen's bedroom. He meant to excuse his behaviour to her, but what he saw prevented that.

For instead of the gorgeously dressed and be-jewelled Virgin Queen he found Elizabeth, still not fully dressed, without her wig or her make-up, toothless, wrinkled and balding, and looking all of her sixty-six years.

As always, she kept her composure admirably. She gave him her hand to kiss, and told him that if he returned later she would see him in private and he could explain himself. Essex seems to have felt that the interview had gone well and departed in high heart to change his clothes and prepare himself for his audience with her. He does not appear to have had any conception of what he had done.

Elizabeth herself seems to have been torn in three directions at least. Her long affection for the Earl meant that she might have felt some genuine pleasure in having him safely back; but that would be mixed with alarm and strong displeasure at his disobedience to her orders and his failure to subdue Tyrone. There was also the intolerable fact that he, whom she had loved, had penetrated behind the splendour of her public mask and seen her as she really was, an old and ugly woman. The absence of mirrors in her apartments meant that Elizabeth no longer knew what she really looked like, but she must have had her suspicions. Now he had insulted her both as a queen and as a woman, and it was not possible that she could feel the same about him as she had done before.

She bided her time, however. That morning she listened to him for an hour and a half, and Essex was sure he had won her round. But that afternoon she saw him again and told him that he must explain himself to the Council, and also gave him to understand that she was still far from happy about his conduct. Finally, late that night, a message came to tell him that he was confined to his chamber. Once, many years ago, Elizabeth had told his stepfather Leicester that her court would have only one mistress and no master. Now Leicester's stepson was being taught the same lesson.

It is possible that Elizabeth still feared that Essex's precipitate return might herald a rebellion, and that confining him to his quarters was meant to test the water. When there was no sign of any unrest, she seems to have decided that it was safe to move decisively, and put him under house arrest, in the care of the Lord Keeper. He was now effectively a prisoner, although he was spared being sent to the Tower. As so often when he was under stress, he became ill, this time seriously. This increased the general popular sympathy for him, but Elizabeth was unmoved: she still forbade even his wife to see him, and a list was read out in the Court of Star Chamber of her complaints against him. Even when he was said to be dying Elizabeth did not relent, although she did pay him a visit to establish whether or not his illness was a genuine one. Things were not improved by the news from Ireland that Tyrone had broken the truce he had induced Essex to agree to.

Gradually, the Earl began to recover from his illness, to face a bleak future. His thoughts turned again to the possibility of a rebellion. He tried to persuade King James of Scotland to help him, but James, knowing that Elizabeth could not live for ever and almost certain that one day he would be King in her place, was reluctant to encourage rebellion against crowned sovereigns, feeling it to be a dangerous precedent. Eventually, Elizabeth began to show signs of relenting; perhaps her genuine affection for Essex was having its effect, or perhaps she felt that his popularity made it dangerous to keep him in disgrace. He was allowed back to his own house, and after an eleven-hour tribunal in which he was told of all his faults he was eventually allowed to go free again. But the Queen was determined to keep a check on his power. She had previously given him the right to make money from the import of certain sorts of wines; now she refused to renew the privilege, keeping the income for herself. Essex was appalled and outraged: his family fortunes had never really recovered from his father's time in Ireland, and now this dealt them a crippling blow. He made an ugly remark about the 'crooked carcase' of the Queen, which was eventually passed back to her; and he began once more to think about rebellion.

He counted on his popularity in the city to win him support, and so he made few plans. He did put about a rumour that Robert Cecil was treacherously intriguing for the Catholic Princess of Spain to be Elizabeth's successor instead of the Protestant King James of Scotland; maybe Essex even

105

believed this, and certainly it might help bring over the staunchly Protestant leaders of the citizens of London to his side. Interestingly, one of his men also went to see the city's leading company of actors to bribe them to put on a play: *Richard II*. Elizabeth had been right to be sensitive on the issue; Essex's followers clearly felt that seeing a king deposed on stage would encourage people to depose a real queen the following day.

His plans, however, had not escaped the attention of Robert Cecil and the Queen, who ordered the guard round the court to be doubled. When he heard this, Essex knew that his original plan of taking the court by surprise was no longer possible. Messengers from Elizabeth arrived at Essex House to ask the Earl for an explanation of his actions, but Essex locked them in the house and set out with his followers—around 300 of them—to appeal to the citizens of London to join him.

He saw no one. A herald had already been sent by Robert Cecil to proclaim Essex and his followers traitors; people had locked themselves into their houses and stared silently through their windows as the Earl's procession passed by. Perhaps for the first time in his life, it was brought home to Essex that however great his personal popularity, the woman who had been their Queen for forty-two years commanded the absolute loyalty of her subjects. He had been wrong in thinking that his mediaeval, aristocratic view of the position of the ruler was still valid; the Tudor myth-making apparatus had worked.

The Essex rebellion was soon over. At Whitehall, Robert Cecil had his work cut out to stop Elizabeth from going out into the streets personally to see if any rebel would dare to face her; but soon he was able to reassure her that such action was quite unnecessary. With some difficulty, Essex had got back to his house and had tried to barricade it against the government troops, but he had soon realized that the position was hopeless and had surrendered. He was sent straight to the Tower of London, and tried for treason. The outcome was a foregone conclusion: a sentence of death. Elizabeth could have pardoned him, but although, with characteristic vacillation, she postponed the execution once, she changed her mind again the next day and allowed it to proceed. Essex had threatened her power as a queen and her self-confidence as a woman; either offence would have been serious enough, and together they were unpardonable. Essex, still not 34, was beheaded on Tower Green, were, sixty-five years before, Elizabeth's mother Anne Boleyn had lost her head.

For the remaining two years of her reign, Elizabeth often appeared to be grieving for him, yet although his death might be a personal tragedy for her, in some ways it represented the crowning achievement of her career. Rebellion had been the bane of the Tudor monarchs, and Elizabeth had devoted much of her energy to projecting so powerful an image of her government that any thoughts of rebellion against her would be strangled at birth. The abject failure of the Essex rebellion showed how well she had succeeded.

The whole career of Essex, indeed, illustrates several points about Elizabeth's method of government and about Elizabethan court culture. One of the main reasons for Essex's discontent was that he was unable to secure appointments and favours for his personal followers. The mechanisms of government in the period were largely founded on a system of patronage; either the rights to posts at court and in the government, and other lucrative appointments or perquisites, were obtained by important noblemen, and given by them to whomever they wished, or, more usually, the Queen would accept nominations from them for such positions. The noblemen's ability to distribute such rewards to their friends meant that people would be eager to follow them, and in the hierarchical world of the Elizabethan court the status and importance of a nobleman were partly determined by how many people were perceived as being his followers. Such a system might seem a ludicrous way of filling important jobs, but in fact it was very much in the interests of the noblemen concerned to maintain their position with the Queen by ensuring that the people they got appointed were actually able to perform their functions, and on the whole the system worked well.

Elizabeth was always careful, however, never to allow a monopoly of patronage to fall into the hands of any one man. If that happened, she herself would be bypassed in the process and so would lose some of her importance, and others would become discontented and find no reason still to remain at court. The success of the Elizabethan court system depended on as many of her nobles as possible finding it worth their while to live in her court, where she could keep an eye on them, rather than retiring to the country where they might begin to stir up trouble for her. So even in the early days of her reign, when Essex's stepfather the Earl of Leicester had appeared to be her undisputed favourite, she had always been careful to keep a countercheck to his power by distributing favours to other people as well; when the French king had offered to bestow the Order of St. Michael on any nobleman of her choice, since being a woman she could not receive it herself, she had asked for him to give it to not one but two of her courtiers, Leicester and her cousin the Duke of Norfolk. She always liked to balance favours to one person or party by favours to another.

This was what Essex could never understand. Although the Queen's policy was in fact to favour his own followers and the Cecils' equally, Essex took every job or perquisite given to a Cecil supporter as a personal insult. But this was his failure, not Elizabeth's. In the reign of her successor, King James I, patronage was for long periods allowed to be concentrated in the hands of one particular favourite: the result was massive discontent, the bringing of the court into disrepute, and, it could be argued, the sowing of some of the seeds of dissatisfaction which eventually led to the English Civil War in the reign of James's son Charles I. It is worth noting that in the Civil War, one of the leaders of the rebel Parliamentary army was the son of Essex. Essex himself, however, had misjudged the political climate of his times; there was no place for his view of the proper relations between sovereign and great lord in the court of Elizabeth. The court system that she had created and the myth and cult she had constructed around herself had triumphed.

VI

The Surroundings of the Court

ELIZABETH inherited from her father King Henry VIII a large number of palaces, most of them within easy reach of London. When the Archduke Charles of Austria was thinking of marrying her, he sent an envoy to England who reported back to him that

> I have seen several very fine summer residences that belong to her . . . and I may say that there are none in the world so richly garnished with costly furniture of silk, adorned with gold, pearls and precious stones. Then she has some twenty other houses, all of which might justly be called royal summer residences. Hence she is well worth the trouble.

Of course Elizabeth would be anxious for such an important envoy to see nothing but what would impress him—we know that on another occasion, when she was receiving ambassadors from Tsar Boris Godunov of Muscovy, a cover was put over the table so that 'the oldness of the board be not seen'—but on the whole the picture painted by the envoy of the Archduke Charles was accurate enough. She was, indeed, well endowed with palaces.

Most centrally, there was Whitehall, which had been built by Cardinal Wolsey and christened by him York Place, after his Archbishopric of York, but which he had given to Henry VIII in a vain attempt to win back the King's favour. Another palace of Elizabeth's which had been originally a gift of Wolsey's, made with the same purpose, had been his magnificent residence of Hampton Court. This could be reached by river from London, as could Richmond Palace, built by her grandfather King Henry VII on the burnt ruins of the old royal Palace of Sheen and named Richmond because he had been Earl of Richmond before he became King; and still further down the Thames were the palace of Oatlands and Windsor Castle, where her father was buried. Close to Whitehall was Greenwich Palace, where Elizabeth herself had been born. Further afield there was the old palace of Woodstock, near Oxford, with its romantic legend of Fair Rosamund, the mistress of Elizabeth's twelfth-century ancestor King Henry II who was said to have been murdered by his jealous wife. Another palace which had come down to Elizabeth from her Plantagenet ancestors was Eltham, near Greenwich, where she had spent time as a baby; and there were also the old palace of Hatfield (where Elizabeth had been brought up and which she gave to her trusted counsellor William Cecil, Lord Burghley), Newhall in Essex and, in Surrey, her father's great palace of Nonsuch, so called because he had built it to be beyond comparison.

There were good reasons for having so many palaces so close together. Travelling through the tightly-packed streets of London and over rough country roads was difficult, so it was a much more attractive prospect to go by river, in the great royal barge: hence the reason for Whitehall, Greenwich, Richmond, Hampton Court, Oatlands and Windsor all being so close to the river Thames. Also, overcrowding and poor sanitary facilities meant that it was virtually impossible to keep a large Elizabethan house clean while there were people still living in it. Owners of a large house would usually have a smaller one in the grounds to which they could retreat once a year or so to keep what was known as 'secret house' while their main residence was being cleaned; owners of more than one property would simply move from house to house. Moreover, since there was no efficient transport or storage of food, if the court stayed too long in one place it might well find itself eating up all the currently available food in that area, so it had long been the custom for great households to move from one to the other of their estates to ensure fresh supplies of produce; and frequent changes of residence further meant that Elizabeth and the splendour of her court could be seen by greater numbers of her people, which would give them a personal focus for loyalty.

Elizabeth was fortunate to inherit so many palaces, because

although the Elizabethan age is often considered to be one of the greatest periods of English architecture, building houses was an expensive business, and the Queen's reluctance to spend money meant that she herself erected none of the great buildings of her reign. When it became apparent that the palace at Whitehall absolutely had to have a new banqueting hall, Elizabeth borrowed the idea used by her father at the Field of the Cloth of Gold and erected what was in effect a glorified tent, with walls of canvas painted to look like stone and thirty 'masts' each forty feet tall to hold it up. In its own way it was very splendid: its perimeter measured 332 feet, it had 292 windows, its walls were decorated with holly, ivy and flowers, its ceiling was decorated with suns, clouds and stars and hanging wicker decorations adorned with exotic fruit, and, a German visitor noted, 'up above in the bushes or the lofty trees there are many birds which sing magnificently.' It also held for Elizabeth the immense attraction that it was far cheaper than an actual building would have been, and took only twenty-four days to erect.

Such stopgaps, however, also had their disadvantages: even with many repairs, the banqueting house lasted only twenty-four years, and had to be replaced in more permanent form by her successor soon after he came to the throne. Also, although a tent might not be too bad when it was used only for banquets and shows, it was less pleasant as accommodation, as many of Elizabeth's long-suffering courtiers found to their cost when they followed the Queen on her annual progresses or to one of the less well-equipped palaces. Although the Queen herself was always properly lodged on such occasions, often the courtiers had to make do with overcrowded lodgings or, worse still, what amounted to campsites. Such conditions led to quarrels and discontent: on one occasion there was a terrible scene when Sir Walter Raleigh commandeered for himself the lodgings reserved for Sir Christopher Hatton, and towards the end of the reign the Queen's champion, Sir Henry Lee, took one look at the tent that had been allotted to him and promptly left the court, saying 'I am old and come now evil away with the inconveniences of progress.' To remedy such situations, however, would cost money, and that Elizabeth, as ever,

111

was not prepared to consider. Even had matters been worse than they were, she might not have been prepared to remedy them; it was, therefore, fortunate that she found herself, in general, so well provided for accommodation, whether she was staying in her own palaces or visiting the houses of her richer subjects on progress.

There were various reasons which had acted together to make the England which Elizabeth had inherited already well stocked with residences capable of receiving a queen. One of the primary causes of the building boom had, in fact, been intimately connected with Elizabeth's own birth. When her father, King Henry VIII, had wanted to marry her mother Anne Boleyn, he had been unable to obtain the consent of the Pope to divorce his first wife in order to do so; he had therefore broken with the Roman Catholic church and, at the same time, had abolished England's many ancient communities of monks and nuns, confiscating their wealth and forcing them to abandon their abbeys, priories and convents. Furthermore, he had known that such radical decisions meant that he risked alienating many of his subjects who still clung to the traditional Catholic faith, and he had decided to ensure the loyalty of many of the most important noble and gentry families by making them presents of land and buildings which had formerly belonged to the monasteries, thus ensuring that they acquired a vested interest in maintaining his new English church, since a reconciliation with Rome would mean that the monasteries would be reinstated and they would therefore lose all the new lands they had acquired.

Many of England's important families thus found themselves not only with large amounts of new land, but also with monastic buildings which could either be converted into houses or could be dismantled and used as sources of valuable building materials. Many of England's great country houses, such as Woburn Abbey in Bedfordshire, still bear names which show that they originated in such uses of monastic lands. Some of them, too, have stories attached to them which also date from the time of their conversion from religious use, and reflect some of the uneasiness generated by these radical changes in English life. In many places, it

112

was rumoured that the monks had cursed the people who had taken their lands from them. The Catholic family of Browne, for instance, inherited the great house of Cowdray from a relative who had received large grants of church land, and were consequently rumoured to have been warned that one day they and the house too would be destroyed by the curse of fire and water. Sure enough, in 1793 the house burned down and the heir to the title was drowned in Germany. His sister's two sons could still have inherited the title—but they, too, drowned, in a sailing accident. The man responsible for the dissolution of the monasteries, Henry VIII himself, seemed to have suffered similar divine retribution when, after his death, his corpse, on its final journey to its tomb, was temporarily deposited at Syon House, which had formerly been a convent of the Bridgettine order. There the processes of putrefaction in the body caused the lid to burst open and part of the king's corpse was eaten by dogs.

It took more than monkish curses, however, to deter Tudor noblemen from taking land and money when the opportunity was offered to them, and the process of converting former abbeys and priories went on apace. And not only were the land and money available, there were also other factors to encourage the building boom. The monastic communities, made wealthy by centuries of donations from the pious, had been constantly repairing and embellishing their properties for the greater glory of God and of their own particular monastic orders, and had consequently been important employers of craftsmen, builders, masons and so forth. The dissolution of the monasteries meant that all these highly skilled workers were suddenly available for secular commissions. Furthermore, recent changes in ways and patterns of living had meant that many families found their old residences were now outmoded or undesirable, and they accordingly made use of the opportunity to build new houses in a new style.

This new style of building had come about for various reasons. Rooms, like everything else, go in and out of fashion, as is shown by the existence in Victorian times of rooms such as breakfast rooms, billiard rooms, day nurseries and night nurseries, and withdrawing rooms for ladies to go to while the men had their port and cigars. In the sixteenth century, rising standards of comfort, elegance and privacy meant that families who could afford it now wanted more rooms than before and for different purposes from before; it had become increasingly unfashionable for the head of the household and his family to eat their meals in a large communal hall along with everybody else, so a dining-parlour was now needed, and new advances in ways of constructing chimneys had also made possible different, more economical arrangements of rooms. Originally, the Norman and early mediaeval type of hall-house had been known as a 'fire house', because their primary function was considered to be places for keeping people warm and dry. Before fireplaces and chimneys were invented fires were lit in the centre of halls, and houses could not have a second storey or a ceiling but had to be open all the way to the roof, which had to have a small hole cut in it so that the smoke from the fire could escape through it—otherwise the people in the house would have been suffocated. An example of such a hall can still be seen at Penshurst Place, in Kent. But gradually, as the principles of fireplaces and of chimneys became increasingly understood, the need for fire no longer had to be the sole requirement in house design, and other considerations could be included as well. It is possible to see the immensely tall and flamboyant chimney stacks which are so often a feature of Tudor buildings as both a statement of the owner's wealth in being able to afford so many fireplaces and the fuel to keep them all going, and also as an expression of power and triumph in this ability to control fire. Indeed, chimneystacks were so much in fashion that sometimes false ones were built onto houses, to give the impression that there were more fireplaces inside than there actually were.

Of the other considerations that had traditionally been important in the construction of dwellings, the most important was often defence. Here, too, the Tudor period was witnessing a change. There had long been a conflict between mediaeval kings and their barons over whether barons should or should not build castles. Castles were status symbols, and they were also, in a country which witnessed frequent fighting, practical necessities for people who could

114

afford them; but they were also seen by kings as a challenge to their authority, and as potentially threatening, because they could be used as strongholds in which rebellious barons could be safe from the King's authority. Consequently laws had been passed making it illegal to fortify a building without the King's consent, although the law was often flouted in times of civil war or during the reign of a weak king.

The first two Tudors, however, were not weak kings, and were certainly not the sort to allow unlicensed castle building. Indeed in the reign of Henry VIII the Duke of Buckingham, when being tried for treason, found himself in trouble for having built something that even *looked* like a castle, though the building in question, Thornbury Castle in Gloucestershire, was in fact so full of large, vulnerable glass windows that it could never have been seriously defensible. Since the Duke of Buckingham lost his head, such cases gave pause for thought. In any case, new developments in artillery during the period were making traditional castles obsolete, and the cramped conditions of castles were also incompatible with the ideas of civilized living which were beginning to filter into England from France and Italy. To build a castle also meant that you had, in effect, not much faith in the present government. Such a gesture was hardly likely to go down well with Henry VII or Henry VIII, and it did, moreover, seem that the troubled times of the Wars of the Roses really had gone for ever. Families whose principal home or homes were castles were increasingly likely to add to the building boom by wanting to build something else.

The final consideration motivating the new style of building was once again the result of new ideas coming out of France and Italy. Not only had patrons and architects in these two countries been stressing increasing comfort and luxury in houses, they had also been following another, related idea about the proper function of houses: that they should impress. As well as just being lived in, the house, the palace and the château could also become important weapons in the battle, so vital to the sixteenth-century mind, to boost one's status, one's public image, and one's projection of one's own importance.

The idea made an especially direct impact in England

because it was adopted in France by King Francis I, and anything done by Francis would soon be copied in England by King Henry VIII, who regarded Francis as a dangerous rival for the position of most splendid and cultured prince in Europe. The French in turn came across the idea in Italy, which they had invaded in the late fifteenth century, and they even imported Italian artists, such as Rosso and Primaticcio who were responsible fcr the decoration of Fontainebleau, to help them put it into practice. Many of the great châteaux of the Loire owe their origins to this period, and Henry VIII's palace of Nonsuch was intended as a direct answer to Francis I's Chambord. Courtiers also began to build houses which were deliberately designed to impress, and although Elizabeth I herself had no intention of spending money on such things, she was more than happy to see her nobles doing so and producing houses which were not only able to accommodate her when she came on progress, but which also functioned as conspicuous demonstrations of the wealth and taste of her followers and of their confidence in a secure, peaceful future for themselves and their families.

Many of the great houses of Elizabethan England survive today to demonstrate the way in which they were used as showpieces of the wealth, taste, status, and even of the wit and learning of their original builders. The very fact that so many people were building great houses at the same time produced an atmosphere of competition, in which courtiers vied to outdo each other in the size and splendour of the individual rooms and of the house overall. One room in particular was the focus of considerable rivalry: the long gallery, an area of the house that was invented during the Tudor period. There had been galleries in earlier houses, but they usually adjoined a garden and were often open to the weather on one side. Since there were no corridors at this period, however, people soon began to realize that a gallery which was completely enclosed within the actual house provided a convenient way of getting from one place to another without having to pass through a sequence of rooms, and that its length also meant that it could be used as a place to walk up and down in, providing exercise, especially for ladies, when the weather was too wet to go outside.

From this it was a logical step to decide that people might as well have something to look at while they were walking up and down; galleries therefore began to be filled with portraits, which it was becoming increasingly fashionable to collect (this use of them is commemorated in our modern term 'art gallery'), and galleries also began to be placed at the top of the house, from where the best view could be obtained. Soon they became a vital feature of any house with pretensions to splendour, and there was great competition amongst builders of houses to have the most impressive long gallery. Montacute House in Somerset had one 170 feet long, but that was soon outdone by Worksop Manor in Derbyshire, where the long gallery was 212 feet long and 36 feet wide; and in turn Lord Dunbar, building in his new house at Berwick shortly after Elizabeth's successor James I had come to the throne, boasted 'that Worksop gallery was but a garret in respect of the gallery that would there be'.

As well as rivalling each other in the length of their galleries, people also attempted to outdo each other in possessing the largest and most impressive collection of portraits to go in their galleries. The Elizabethan age was obsessed with genealogy and pedigree, and no great family could be content without as many pictures as possible of important people, living and dead, whom they could claim were either related to them or were friends of theirs or their families, though nothing could upstage in this respect a portrait on the ceiling of the Tiltyard Gallery at Elizabeth's palace of Whitehall—it was of Moses, and was said to be a very good likeness!

Long galleries also afforded yet another means for the display of status and wealth: the fact that one of their important features was the view from them meant that they necessarily had to have a lot of windows, and the glass that went in those windows was, in Elizabethan England, an expensive commodity, so the more of it your house displayed, the wealthier you must therefore be. The wall of the gallery at Worksop was therefore made up almost entirely of windows, as a means of impressing on all who saw it the wealth of its builder. Even when there was no long gallery, it was still fashionable to have as many windows as possible and to make them as large as possible. When Elizabeth's favourite Robert Dudley, Earl of Leicester, was making alterations to his castle at Kenilworth in preparation for receiving the Queen, the original mediaeval shape and structure of the buildings meant that it was impossible for him to insert a long gallery anywhere, but he nevertheless ensured that the buildings were studded with large windows. Not only was the amount of glass in these a status symbol in itself, but he could also demonstrate his wealth still further by filling all available rooms, every evening, with candles, which, because the Elizabethans did not use curtains, would mean that his house would shine out like a beacon far into the night. Candles were expensive and were normally used very sparingly indeed; such conspicuous consumption of them advertised Leicester's status as a great nobleman and a favourite of the Queen. Other nobles also made ostentatious use of glass and candles in this way, and the houses they built became known as 'lantern houses', because in the dark nights before the age of street lamps the light they generated could be seen far and wide.

It was, then, easy for the Elizabethan nobleman to use his house to proclaim his wealth; the use of windows and candles, and sometimes the use of expensive materials such as marble, meant that a house could be 'read' almost like a bank statement by observers at the time. But money was not all that was required to ensure a satisfactory image for a nobleman or a wealthy courtier; since the reign of Elizabeth's grandfather King Henry VII influences from the learned, sophisticated courts of Renaissance Italy had been making themselves increasingly felt in England, and it was increasingly imperative for the courtier to show that he was intelligent and cultured as well as rich. Baldessare Castiglione's *The Courtier* had provided a terrifying list of the accomplishments and talents needed to be a successful courtier, and even if few Elizabethans felt up to emulating Castiglione's ideal man, they were nevertheless often anxious to show that they were aware of current ideas, or were, at least, following current fashions.

This meant that the builders of the great Elizabethan

houses were usually keen to use their houses to display their culture, erudition and knowledge of the latest thinking in architecture. At Nonsuch, for instance, Elizabeth's father King Henry VIII had imported French and Italian artists to provide fashionably classical decoration in paint and stucco of the main facades: a figure of Henry VIII himself was portrayed sitting on his throne and surrounded by the gods of Olympus and the labours of Hercules, the apartments intended for the Queen were decorated with allegorical figures representing the qualities appropriate to women in both the classical and the Christian traditions (perhaps Henry felt it would bring him better luck with his wives), and the whole was topped by portraits of thirty-one Roman emperors, including Julius Caesar who, though not in fact an Emperor, was much admired and had played a part in the history of Britain. Similarly the great house of Theobalds, built by Elizabeth's minister William Cecil, Lord Burghley, had decorative schemes featuring not only pedigrees of Burghley himself and of his friends, but also fresco paintings after the Italian fashion.

Not only fresco painting, but almost all of the most important new ideas came from Italy. But they were often filtered through to England via the Low Countries or France; and partly because of this and partly for other reasons, the form in which they were eventually adopted in England was very often radically different from the form in which they had originated in Italy. Henry VIII's Reformation of the English Church had done much to cut England off from direct contact with the still-Catholic continent; most of the few Englishmen who had ever ventured abroad either came back of their own accord or were recalled, and England soon became isolated from the artistic developments taking place in Italy. Furthermore, some Italian architectural practices were simply unsuited to England, because of the difference in climate. The great Italian architect Andrea Palladio might not have to worry unduly about heating the villas he designed in the area around Venice, particularly if they were meant primarily for use in the summer; it was a very different matter for Englishmen trying to follow Palladian principles in architecture, and the problem of where to put the chimneystacks so

119

necessary in the English climate but so unsuited to the lines of the Palladian house was still troubling people well into the eighteenth century (an ingenious solution can be seen at Chiswick House in London, built in the eighteenth century by Lord Burlington, where the chimneystacks are disguised as classical obelisks).

Fortunately for them, however, Englishmen of the sixteenth century did not actually realize the full seriousness of the problem with which they were faced, for they regarded the ideas of Palladian architecture, and the variations on Italian architecture developed in the Low Countries and France, as a repertory of patterns and decorative ideas that could be, as it were, 'mixed and matched', from which selected motifs or ornament could be taken and interspersed at will with traditional elements of English houses that dated back to mediaeval times. They failed to grasp that Palladian architecture was in fact based on what were considered to be firm and unalterable rules, originally laid down by the revered Roman architect Vitruvius and rediscovered and reinterpreted by Palladio, and with gay abandon they broke all the rules by applying classical pilasters in the wrong sequence or the wrong place, with the wrong entablature or with no entablature at all, or mixed with older, mediaeval ideas. Earlier in the century, the Duke of Somerset, Lord Protector for part of the reign of Elizabeth's brother King Edward VI, had built a more truly classical house on the Strand, but, possibly because the Lord Protector had soon afterwards lost his head, the style had not caught on. The Elizabethans preferred their own eclectic mixtures, which, although technically incorrect, often give their houses great charm and vibrancy.

Many of the elements which they liked to intermix with the classical were derived from the architecture of castles. Classical pillars and pilasters, friezes and roundels might show their erudition, but, in what was for England a much older vocabulary than that of classical architecture, elements drawn from the castle signified strength and status. They had no desire to convey feelings of insecurity or danger by building anything that could possibly be mistaken for a real castle, but many of their buildings, like Wollaton

120

in Nottinghamshire, playfully combine visual allusions to castles, such as battlements, turrets and the square shape of a castle keep, with vast amounts of glass which would make it quite indefensible in real warfare. The same idea can be seen at a house built five years after Elizabeth's death by her minister Robert Cecil, Cranborne Manor in Dorset, where genuine buttresses from a real thirteenth-century castle were decorated with classical pilasters. Many other houses incorporated similar elements, so that the spectators who gazed at them could read them not only as signifying wealth, status, culture and learning, but would be led, too, to associate their owners with the traditions of Arthurian and mediaeval chivalry which Elizabethan courtiers liked to think of themselves as reviving. Houses built like castles could also serve to suggest that their occupiers possessed the added social advantage of springing from ancient families with long traditions of wealth and chivalry.

As well as these general signals, some people wished their houses to give out more specific messages. The Elizabethan mind adored what it called 'conceits' or 'devices'—complicated puzzles with hidden meanings, which worked something on the principle of crossword clues and could take either verbal or visual form. They eagerly devoured books of 'emblems', an emblem being a riddling picture with verses underneath explaining it; they appeared at tournaments with complicated devices on their shields which had to be interpreted by the spectators; their portraits featured objects with allegorical significances—Sir Thomas More's daughter, for instance, had herself painted standing on a tortoise, famous for its slowness, to signify that a good woman should never venture far from home. Part of the appeal held by the device for the Elizabethans was that they felt it expressed both the taste and wit of the person who invented it and also the intelligence of the person who could successfully interpret it, and so was satisfactory to both parties. The 'device' or 'conceit' proved enduringly popular, and people delighted in finding new applications for it.

One such application was house design. In a way it was a sort of device to have a house which looked like a castle without actually being one; and other, more complex and more individual devices could also be used. The Catholic Sir Thomas Tresham, for instance, decided to give outward expression to his religion by building two houses which would actually be inherently Catholic in design and in ornamentation: Rushton Triangular Lodge and Lyveden New Bield, both in Northamptonshire. Both these houses were meant to be clearly readable as public proclamations of their owner's adherence to Catholicism and as architectural expressions of particular Catholic doctrines.

The Triangular Lodge at Rushton was built by Sir Thomas for the man who looked after his rabbit warrens. (Rabbits, first introduced to England by the Normans for food, were popular for eating.) As its name suggests, the lodge was built in the form of a triangle, each of its sides being thirty-three and a third feet long, so that the total length of its sides was exactly 100 feet. There had long been an interest in Italian architecture in constructing churches in the shapes of perfect geometrical forms as a way of expressing the perfection of God: the circular church designs of Leonardo da Vinci and the fondness of architects like Bramante, Michelangelo and Raphael for designs incorporating perfect circles, cubes and hemispheres are illustrations of this. Tresham's Lodge is clearly related to this idea, but the use of the triangular shape enabled him to imbue it with additional significance in that the three sides making up the perfect whole of 100 feet formed an apt expression of the three persons of the Father, the Son and the Holy Ghost making up the unity of the Holy Trinity. Perhaps there was also a further reference to Sir Thomas's own name, since his surname Tresham contained the Latin word 'tres', meaning three.

The pattern of threes was continued throughout the building: there were three storeys, with three windows (divided into three) on each storey and three gables above them, and on each side there was an inscription about the Trinity, composed of exactly thirty-three letters (thirty-three, as well as being a combination of threes, was also the age of Christ at the time of His death, and was therefore a doubly meaningful number). The building was also adorned with reliefs of motifs like the pelican pecking at her own breast to feed her young ones with the drops of her blood, a symbol of Christ giving His own body and blood in the Eucharist and thus a reference to the Catholic doctrine of the Real Presence. Whatever the man who looked after the rabbits may have thought about it all, the message of the building would have been clear to all who looked at it.

Ten years later Sir Thomas was building again, at Lyveden New Bield, though this time he died before he could finish the work and it is now a ruin. Like the Triangular Lodge, Lyveden New Bield was intended as a visibly Catholic piece of architecture. It may have been intended as the sort of small lodge to which a family retired when they were keeping 'secret house' while their main house was being cleaned, or perhaps it was meant as a sort of glorified summer-house. But although it is difficult to determine what its practical purpose was, its allegorical message is clear. It was a description in stone of the Passion of Christ, and also contained references to the Virgin as Our Lady of Sorrows.

It was built in the form of a cross, and again it was based on numbers. Sir Thomas felt that the number five signified the Salvation (possibly because of the five wounds, in His hands, His feet and His side, received by Christ on the cross), and therefore the building was made up of five equal squares, one in the middle and one projecting from each side. Each of these four projecting squares terminates not in a flat wall but in a five-sided bay, of which each side is five feet long. Like the Triangular Lodge, the building is three storeys high (again alluding to the Trinity), with three windows on each side, and once more there are inscriptions running round the building, this time in praise of Christ and of the Virgin; also the inscriptions were to be made up of eighty-one letters, since eighty-one is nine times nine and the Tresham coat of arms featured three flower-like devices with three leaves each, making nine in total. The building was further decorated with representations of the seven symbols of the Passion of Christ, the pillar, the ladder, the cross, the crown of thorns, the sponge, the spear, and the S-shaped scourge with which He was whipped. All this must have taken immensely careful planning, but Sir Thomas had plenty of leisure: fifteen years of his life were spent either in prison or

123

under house arrest, sometimes as a result of financial arguments with relatives but more often because of his Catholic faith, which he resolutely refused to renounce and which he took the opportunity of advertising so unmistakably in these two buildings.

Sir Thomas was not the only Elizabethan to produce architectural 'conceits', though his are among the most elaborate. To erect such buildings was, for one thing, yet another way of demonstrating your surplus wealth; to treat the expensive business of architecture as a suitable medium for a joke must mean that your resources were definitely not stretched. Not everybody could afford to do this, and in fact there have come down to us several designs for such buildings which, often for financial reasons, were never built, such as the architect John Thorpe's plan for a house in the shape of his own initials, I (for Ioannes) and T, joined together. Other houses, however, were built; such was the anxiety of Elizabethans to give visible outward expression to their status, their learning and, in some cases, their personalities or affiliations. There are houses based on the shape of the letter Y (possibly another emblem of the Trinity, since three separate elements join to make one letter, and also the capital form of the first letter of the Greek word for the Son); there are houses in the shape of a pentagon (perhaps because its five sides represented the five wounds of Christ, or perhaps just as a display of wit), houses in the shape of a Greek cross (of which the significance is unclear), and, most popular of all, there are innumerable houses in the shape of an E: in some cases because Elizabethan house planning made an E a particularly convenient shape; in other cases, we are told, because E was the first letter of 'Emmanuel', a name for God, and also because E was of course the first letter of 'Elizabeth', so that an E-shaped house represented a way of expressing one's devotion to the Queen. This obsession with conceits and devices even meant that when, early in the seventeenth century, an English architect, Inigo Jones, finally travelled to Italy, mastered the principles of Palladian architecture and the rules of harmony, order and proportion on which it was based and built a truly Palladian house in England, courtiers used to the traditions of Elizabethan architecture simply could not understand what was going on, and devoted many fruitless hours to trying to read into it some allegorical meaning.

The buildings in which the court of Elizabeth was accustomed to pass its time, therefore, served many purposes other than the strictly functional. Indeed convenience often ran a very poor second to considerations of display: instead of the rambling houses of the late mediaeval and early Tudor period, it now became fashionable to build compact, symmetrical houses, and on one occasion Sir Nicholas Bacon rebuked his brother-in-law, Elizabeth's minister William Cecil, for sacrificing comfort and even hygiene to symmetry by putting a lavatory 'too near the lodging, too near an oven, and too near a little larder'. Sir Nicholas felt that Cecil 'had been better to have offended your eye outward than your nose inward'. But Sir Nicholas was here showing himself to be out of step with the spirit of the times. Symmetry was considered to be impressive, so symmetry there had to be; galleries needed to be long, so houses were stretched to accommodate them; there was a fashion for little banqueting-houses, sometimes in the grounds but more often on roofs, to which people could go to admire the view and to take fruit and wine after dinner, so the skylines of great Elizabethan mansions promptly developed tiny turreted banqueting-houses. In the Elizabethan house the Elizabethan concern with the conscious creation of an image finds full expression.

The same was true of the Elizabethan garden. Gardens had been an important feature of English houses since Roman times at least: they were important sources of food, and they also had important symbolic significances. They represented man's control over the forces of nature, and, for Christian cultures, each garden was also a reminder and, in a small way, an attempted recreation of the first garden of all, the Garden of Eden.

It is easy to overlook the importance of gardens in Elizabethan times, since garden designs are by their very nature ephemeral and easily changed or destroyed. In gardening as in everything else fashions change, and whereas some families fell on hard times and could not have afforded to rebuild or alter the houses bequeathed to them by their Elizabethan ancestors, it was both simple and cheap to replant one's garden. It was less simple and less cheap to adopt the principles of landscape design put forward in the eighteenth and nineteenth centuries by 'Capability' Brown and Humphry Repton, but their ideas became so much the rage that the grounds of many great houses were completely transformed under their influence. Although it has become fashionable since the beginning of the twentieth century to produce recreations of mediaeval and Elizabethan gardens, not a single English garden actually survives from those periods. There are, however, enough illustrations and written descriptions of Elizabethan gardens, and enough known about garden theory of the time, to make possible some sort of sense of how a great Elizabethan garden was organized and how it, too, could be used as a showcase for the wealth, learning, wit, or even the political, personal or religious affiliations of its owner.

One of the major differences between gardens then and now was in the rôle of flowers in the Elizabethan garden. Certainly the Elizabethans grew flowers, but they tended to be interested in them not for their own sake but for the various purposes to which they could be put. Bad smells were considered to be causes of disease, so people often carried nosegays with them, or filled pomanders or bowls with dried sweet-smelling petals. It was also common to use flowers in cooking or for medicinal purposes, and books of the period are full of useful advice about how to make rosewater to flavour pies or how rose petals are good for the heart and mind. In particular it was believed that diseases of specific parts of the body could be cured by plants which were of similar shape to the part of the body concerned; this was known as the 'Doctrine of Signatures' and had been put forward early in the sixteenth century by the famous German doctor Paracelsus.

Finally, flowers were commonly regarded as being symbolic of various qualities or emotions: roses, as now, meant love, and were also the flower of the Virgin Mary; violets stood for fidelity; sunflowers were symbols of faith and loyalty since they turned their heads to follow the

126

sun; pansies indicated thought because their name was derived from the French 'pensée', meaning a thought; lilies meant purity; and so forth. The idea is nicely illustrated in *Hamlet*, where Ophelia, who has gone mad, distributes flowers to her brother, the King and the Queen: rosemary for remembrance, pansies for thoughts, fennel and columbine for unfaithfulness, rue for repentance, and daisies for unrequited love. She would, she says, add violets, the flowers of fidelity, but they are all withered—signifying that there is no fidelity left in the court of Denmark. Similarly, Elizabethans are often shown in their portraits carrying flowers, intended to suggest that they themselves possess the virtues or attributes of that particular flower, or, occasionally, that they are in love with a lady who is symbolized by the flower.

For all these reasons the Elizabethans cultivated flowers in their gardens. They could be picked for use in medicines or food, and they themselves or their plucked petals could be used to decorate houses and make them smell sweet. Flowers which had a particularly attractive smell could be clustered together to make the garden a paradise of scent; sometimes sweet-smelling herbs and small flowers were even planted in areas that were meant to be walked over, so that the family and their friends could crush them as they walked, releasing the scent and steeping their shoes and the hems of their long clothes in a perfume which would help ward off the less pleasant smells that they might encounter elsewhere. (Some impression of how rich the scents of such a garden must have been can be obtained from visiting a reconstructed Tudor garden, such as that at the Tudor House Museum in Southampton, in summertime.) Flowers were valued much less for their own sake than for their practical uses such as these, and also because of their symbolic language, for thanks to that the very flowers in a courtier's garden could promote his constant quest to cultivate and display his image of himself.

The flower most commonly used for this purpose was the rose. Part of the Tudor myth-making initiated by Elizabeth's grandfather, King Henry VII, had centred on the Tudor Rose. For thirty years before Henry VII's accession, England

127

had been in the grip of civil war between the two royal houses of Lancaster and York, each of which claimed the throne. We now know that series of battles as the Wars of the Roses; but that was not, in fact, the name given to them at the time. It was Tudor myth-makers who put out the story that, one day in the garden of the Temple law courts in London, the House of Lancaster had decided to take as its badge a red rose and the House of York a white, and it was Shakespeare's version of the episode in his *Henry VI, Part 1*, which fixed the idea in the popular mind. The great charm of the story, from the Tudor point of view, was that it enabled them to present the marriage between Henry VII, who claimed descent from the house of Lancaster, and his wife Elizabeth, eldest daughter of a Yorkist king, in satisfying symbolic terms as the union of the red rose and the white into the double Tudor rose, which had petals of both colours. This formed such an attractive and distinctive badge that the Tudors made lavish use of it (it appears on places as diverse as the decoration of King's College Chapel, Cambridge, brought to completion by Henry VII and Henry VIII, and the uniforms of the Yeomen of the Guard, instituted by Henry VII).

Elizabeth, too, used the Tudor rose as a badge, and she also linked herself yet more closely with the flower by adopting one variety of it, the eglantine, a single rose with five petals, as one of her own especial symbols. The rose cult of Elizabeth had a complex symbolic meaning. As well as its obvious associations with the Tudor rose, roses had also been the flower traditionally connected with the Virgin Mary, and so for Elizabeth too to be linked with them fitted admirably into the attempt to project herself as a psychological substitute for the Virgin. Roses were also, of course, symbols of love and beauty, which suited the presentation of Elizabeth as a paragon of beauty with whom all her subjects were in love; and the thorns which surround them provided an apt symbol for the fierce resolution of her virginity, preventing the rose from being picked.

So the rose became the flower of Elizabeth, the Virgin Queen, and her courtiers could declare their allegiance to her by planting their gardens with roses. Those who were

128

closest to her and knew the finer details of the cult could simultaneously please Elizabeth and advertise their privileged status as intimates of the Queen by referring to her in more specific detail as the eglantine, as Sir Robert Cecil did in a garden which he created for one of Elizabeth's visits to his father's house at Theobalds; it consisted of a knot-garden cᶜ the Virtues, represented by roses, the Graces, signified by pansies, and nine other flowers representing the Muses, all surrounding an arbour of eglantine, which, the gardener told Elizabeth, was a plant so deeply rooted in the soil that even 'the sun of Spain at the hottest cannot parch it', a reference to the defeat of the Armada three years previously. Such a garden served as a graceful compliment to Elizabeth at the same time as it demonstrated its creator's familiarity with the mythology of the court and his skill, wealth and imagination in being able to produce it.

Another aspect of the cult of the Virgin Mary which could be adapted for use in the gardens of Elizabethan England was the idea of the *hortus conclusus*, the walled or enclosed garden which acted as a symbol of the chastity of the Virgin—the garden signifying her womb, and the walls around its impenetrability. The walled garden had already been adopted as a personal symbol in the previous century by the Duchess Isabella of Portugal, wife of Duke Philip the Good of Burgundy, and now it could be used as a further way of complimenting the Queen. Furthermore, like the growing of roses, which were attractive, sweet-smelling and useful in cooking and medicine, enclosed gardens also made good horticultural sense, for their walls provided shelter from winds for delicate plants and for people walking in them, and could also be used as supports for climbing plants. Because of this walled gardens were already popular, but now they acquired an additional importance.

Apart from growing flowers and building walls, however, there were also other things which could be done in gardens and which could be turned to good account in displaying the position or personality of its creator. In the time of Elizabeth's father Henry VIII it had become fashionable to lay out plants and flowers in 'knots', complicated patterns which could function as demonstrations of ingenuity or, occasionally, vehicles for allegory; and where there were knots there was often a mound, a small artificial hill which provided exercise and a place from which to view the patterns of the knots to best advantage, and which could also carry through the mock-castle theme of many houses by alluding to the defensive mounds on which castles had originally been built. Mounds and knot gardens remained popular throughout the Elizabethan period, as did another feature of Henry VIII's gardens: topiary, the cutting of hedges into decorative shapes (there are particularly impressive examples of topiary gardens still to be seen at Levens Hall in Cumbria and at Packwood House in Warwickshire, where the garden may have been designed not long after the Elizabethan period). The Roman writer Pliny had recorded that the Romans were fond of topiary in their gardens, and so learned and wealthy men of the Italian Renaissance, anxious to imitate classical models as closely as possible, had duly set about creating topiary work in their own gardens.

The results achieved could be spectacular: the garden of the Florentine Rucellai family boasted not only topiary men, women, animals and buildings but also a topiary Pope with his topiary cardinals, while the Medici, rulers of Florence, had in their garden topiary elephants, a topiary ship, and a topiary wolf fleeing from topiary dogs. Some of the elements of the Medici garden may also have been derived from the stories of the Roman writer Ovid's *Metamorphoses*, giving the owners of the garden a chance to display their classical learning as well as their ingenuity. The idea had caught on in England, and at Hampton Court Henry VIII had created a topiary garden which included men, women, flowers, and centaurs, figures from classical mythology supposed to be half man and half horse, which enabled Henry to demonstrate his acquaintance with classical learning.

King Henry's garden at Hampton Court had also included another feature designed to proclaim his status: a series of wooden pillars painted green and white and topped by animals such as lions, greyhounds, dragons and unicorns. The significance of these was that green and white were the livery colours of the Tudors—the colours in which they dressed their servants and by which their followers and possessions could be identified—and the animals were all used by ancestors of the royal family as heraldic supporters, that is, as figures standing on either side of the shield when their coat of arms was displayed in full. The point was made even more plain by the fact that all the heraldic beasts carried a shield upon which the Tudor coat of arms was displayed, and the railings surrounding the garden were painted in green and white. Perhaps part of the reason for the display was that Henry was trying to stamp his own mark on Hampton Court: it once belonged to his minister Cardinal Wolsey, whom Henry considered had grown dangerously over-powerful and had therefore disgraced. Part of the message of the garden, therefore, may have been that Hampton Court now belonged clearly and unmistakably to the King, and that the King was a person of too much power to be trifled with. The same idea was also introduced in the gardens at Whitehall, with the arms and badges suitably updated from King Henry's to Elizabeth's own.

The gardens at Whitehall also contained a trick fountain, of the sort that had once been so popular at the splendid court of Burgundy and was now all the rage in Italy. Indeed fountains in general were playing an increasingly prominent part in Elizabethan gardens; Richmond had a very large one ornamented with lions (which featured in the coats of arms of English Kings), dragons (the symbol of Wales) and red roses, while Nonsuch, which had been originally intended as a hunting base like its French model of Chambord, had a fountain with figures of Diana, the goddess of hunting, turning Actaeon into a stag as a punishment for having seen her bathing naked. Diana was a particularly appropriate choice, because she was a virgin goddess of great beauty, and so Elizabeth herself was often referred to or represented as Diana; and in case any one should doubt the reference, on an arch nearby were two more of Elizabeth's symbols: the pelican, the bird which was supposed to sacrifice for its children and therefore suggested that Elizabeth sacrificed herself for her subjects, and the phoenix, which reproduced itself, without mating, by dying in flames and rising again, and so offered a reassurance that although Elizabeth was a virgin, there was no cause to worry about the succession. There was also a fountain in the garden which the Earl of Leicester created at his castle of Kenilworth, this time of marble, very intricately decorated with shells, fish, including whales, and whirlpools, while real fish swam in its basin. As with so many Elizabethan fountains, however, it was inadvisable to admire it for too long: someone who was familiar with the secrets of the garden was sure to catch sight of you and turn the hidden stopcock which would drench you.

Including in one's garden fountains which would give unwary visitors a soaking was not just a form of practical joke. Just as the Elizabethan love of chimneypots can be seen as directly related to their pleasure in being able to control the potentially dangerous element of fire, and just as all gardens in some sense represented man's ability to order and organize wild nature, so fountains can be interpreted as demonstrating man's power over water. There had certainly been a strong element of this in the gardens created in Spain by its Moorish conquerors; coming from lands bordered by deserts and prone to drought, they had regarded water as the key to life and, rejoicing at finding so much of it in Spain, had filled their gardens there with fountains and ornamental ponds. But as well as indicating power over water, trick fountains also represented, less specifically, a more abstract power over the forces of nature which, to the Elizabethan mind, perhaps hovered on the border of being a form of magic.

The Elizabethan period was a time of deep interest in magic. On one level there was still considerable popular belief in witchcraft: people, the overwhelming majority of them women, continued to be tried and killed as witches, and many people, particularly in the countryside, were still ready to attribute illnesses in themselves or their animals to malevolent neighbours, and to be suspicious of elderly, ugly women with pet animals. In the neighbouring kingdom of Scotland, the King himself, James VI, claimed on more than one occasion to be the victim of witches' plots, and wrote a book on the subject, and when he eventually succeeded Elizabeth as King James VI of Scotland and James I of England his interest in the subject brought about a rash of writings on the subject, of which the most famous is Shakespeare's *Macbeth*. But magic in the wider sense consisted of more than just witchcraft. True magic was understood to be something much grander, nobler, and more intellectual, and was indeed considered to be a way of understanding more clearly the purposes of God and the mystic structure of the universe; and as such it was undoubtedly 'white magic', beneficial rather than harmful, and its practitioners were usually safe from the unpleasant consequences facing those who were thought to be witches.

True magic was primarily based on numbers. Ever since Pythagoras had discovered the mathematical ratios behind musical consonances, philosophers had been attempting to use them to discover what they took to be the mysterious and harmonious proportions behind the structure of the universe. Such a search made perfect sense to philosophers then and later, because it was believed that the whole universe was held together by music in the form of the 'Music of the Spheres'—music believed to be created by the planets, in what was seen as their perpetual 'dance' through the skies, and which could not be heard because man's Fall in the Garden of Eden had made him deaf to the sublime harmonies of the universe. Perhaps, however, the correct interpretation and application of Pythagoras's discoveries could help philosophers decipher the unheard music of the spheres and move closer to an understanding of the universe and of God. It is this sort of attitude to the mystic significance of numbers that underpins Sir Thomas Tresham's planning of his houses around the numbers of three, five, seven and nine.

Along with the fascination with numbers went a deep interest in languages, sometimes manifested as a search for the language of Heaven or for the language spoken on Earth before the Tower of Babel led to the existence of many, fragmented languages. Scholars scanned mystical writings like the *Kabbala* or the writings of the 'Hermetic' school (Hermes had been the Greek god of writing and of messages and his name had therefore been adopted by a writer of the classical world who had called himself Hermes Trismegistus, 'Hermes the Thrice-Wise'); and there was also an interest in codes and in secret forms of writing. Very many people

133

were prepared to regard these enterprises with the utmost seriousness, while other people were attracted by the likely practical results; one of the ways in which some magicians attempted to see if they had the clue to the fundamental structure of the universe was by attempting to change the structure of individual items, most notably by changing base metal into gold.

The high intellectual status of magic and its possible rewards meant that it, too, became something that an Elizabethan courtier might perhaps wish to cultivate as part of his image. One of Elizabeth's favourites, Sir Walter Raleigh, was particularly closely associated with it, and a small group formed round him, one of whom, the Earl of Northumberland, became known as 'The Wizard Earl' for the many experiments he performed. Shakespeare's Prospero, in *The Tempest*, is an example of the sort of white magician in whose existence many Elizabethans might at least half-believe; Prospero bears some resemblance to a real Elizabethan magician, Dr. John Dee, who was invited by Elizabeth I to name the most suitable date for her coronation, became internationally famous and was invited to the court of the Holy Roman Emperor Rudolf at Prague, and has left fascinating accounts of the long conversations he believed himself to have had with various angelic spirits.

All this may seem a very long way indeed from gardening. In fact, however, as English visitors to the continent were already beginning to report, the gardens of Italy and France were proving to be fertile ground for the display of devices whose ingeniousness made them seem almost magical: automata, mechanical birds, animals, musical instruments or figures or tableaux of figures which could execute movements which might seem simple in our own day but were a source of wonder to the eyes of the sixteenth century. In the reign of Elizabeth's successor, James I, such devices would be actually imported into England; meanwhile, the trick fountains of Elizabethan gardens, like so many aspects of Elizabethan gardens, could already serve to tell of their owner's interests, learning and awareness of current fashions, in a language which would be clearly understood by those cultivated visitors whose opinion mattered.

VII

The Court on Progress

ONE of the most notable innovations of Elizabeth I was her habit of taking her court on progress. It had long been traditional for the court to move around a great deal; palaces needed to be cleaned, and there were also a number of reasons why it was desirable for the ruler to show himself in as many parts of his dominions as he could get to. It enabled him to keep an eye on what his barons were up to; it kept him informed about the state of his country; it gave him new areas to hunt and hawk in; and in the early period, when it was still the king's personal responsibility to supply justice when he was called upon to do so, it gave him an opportunity to hear cases and right wrongs—which could also give him a useful popularity boost.

In Elizabeth's case, there was a combination of these traditional reasons and of new motives of her own. Monarchs no longer administered justice in person, but she was as fond as her royal predecessors had been of hunting; she needed to move when there was plague in the area (and London was considered to be generally unhealthy in the summer months) or when her palaces had to be cleaned (or 'sweetened' as it was called); she liked to see what was going on in her country; and, more important still, she also liked to *be* seen. A ruler who was a mere name to her subjects might find that, in a case of conflict, their loyalty went not to her but to their own local lord whom they knew personally; and the risk of that happening might be all the greater when the ruler was not a king, as traditionally, but a queen, a mere woman. Locally based rebellions had been the one great threat to the stability and survival of the Tudor dynasty. There had been one as recently as the reign of Elizabeth's sister Mary, and many of Elizabeth's efforts were devoted to ensuring that it should not happen in her own reign: the failure of the Essex rebellion is a measure of her success. She seems to have felt that her magnificent appearance, enhanced by the presence of her retinue of handsome, well-dressed courtiers, and her undoubted personal charm would help her win the hearts of as many of her subjects as could see her, and in this she appears to have been right.

All these, then, were reasons for keeping up the tradition of moving the court from place to place. Elizabeth, however, made the whole business much more systematic, deliberately devoting the summer months of successive years to travelling as far as possible in as many directions as possible. She also introduced a major refinement to the whole concept of taking the court from residence to residence. Traditionally, the monarch had gone from one to another of his own palaces, where he and his court could live on the produce of his own crown lands. Elizabeth, however, greatly preferred not to stay at her own palaces. Instead, she and her entire court would descend on the house of one of her subjects to be lodged, fed and entertained.

From the point of view of the Queen herself, it was, of course, a masterstroke. It saved her endless trouble; her hosts would feel obliged to give her the best treatment that they possibly could, especially if a subtle or, if necessary, not-so-subtle hint were dropped that she had enjoyed herself more somewhere else; and she was invariably given an expensive parting gift: when she visited Lord Keeper Puckering at Kew she got a fan with diamonds in its handle, a pair of virginals to play on, some clothes, and a jewelled nosegay worth £400, a considerable sum in sixteenth-century terms, and when she went to the house of Sir Julius Caesar she was presented with an embroidered dress of silver cloth, a black cloak with real gold on it, a flowered taffeta hat and a jewel made of gold, rubies and diamonds. As an added bonus, having to bear the cost of entertaining her and her courtiers would also ensure that none of her subjects could become so wealthy as to be able to finance a rebellion against her. It did not in fact save her much money: Lord Burghley calculated that going on progress cost her about £1,000 a year, because although

136

the court was fed by its hosts, it still had to carry with it food for when it was en route, and food cost more in the country—but that, as far as Elizabeth was concerned, was a factor easily outweighed by its manifold advantages.

Matters were rather different for her courtiers and nobles. The business of going on progress meant a tremendous upheaval: wherever she went the Queen would take with her her own bed (which could be dismantled and re-assembled), her most important personal furniture and tapestries, and between 300 and 400 carts full of other baggage, together with an estimated 2,400 horses which all had to be stabled and fed. There was also a problem that Elizabeth was prone to changing her mind about where she was going on progress: on one occasion a carter, having had his orders changed three times in the same morning, said 'Now I see that the Queen is a woman as well as my wife', only to find that the Queen herself had heard him through an open window, and was simultaneously calling him a villain and throwing down some money for him. Even when the court was finally under way and its direction had been determined, those who accompanied the Queen on progress to the houses of her subjects often found that there was not enough room for them all and that they had to lodge in very cramped and uncomfortable conditions; and for the richer courtiers, there was always the possibility that their house might be the next on the Queen's list.

This was a prospect that was regarded in varying ways. Some people were positively eager for the honour of enter-taining their Queen: her friend Lady Norris was very angry when the Earl of Leicester tried to persuade the Queen not to stay at the Norrises' house on progress, and Sir Christopher Hatton in particular was tremendously anxious for her to come and stay with him. Since he knew by experience that houses were often too small to accommodate the whole court in comfort, he permanently ruined his finances by building Holdenby House in Northamptonshire, built on the scale of a palace and a close second in size to the largest house of the age, Lord Burghley's Theobalds. For ten years Sir Christopher tried in vain to persuade the Queen to come and stay in his splendid new house, built especially for her—and then he died. The house was so vast that the upkeep of it proved impossible to handle, and it did not last out the seventeenth century.

Many courtiers and nobles, however, would have envied Sir Christopher for never being visited by the Queen. William More of Loseley, a descendant of Sir Thomas More, persuaded a friend at court to convince the Queen that his house was too small to be visited, but Elizabeth was a difficult woman to put off: the next year she visited him anyway, whether his house was too small or not. Similarly, the Earl of Bedford was very anxious that if Elizabeth absolutely had to come and visit him at Woburn, she should at least not stay any longer than a day and two nights. Some courtiers, however, just decided to make the best of it. Lord Burghley found that each of the queen's visits to his house at Theobalds cost him what was for those days the enormous sum of £3,000 (and she came thirteen times), but he nevertheless set himself to enlarging it to accommodate her until it became the largest house in England.

Sometimes a courtier or a nobleman who was in disgrace might seize the opportunity of a royal visit to try to reingratiate himself: when the queen visited the Earl of Hertford's house at Elvetham he spared no expense to try to please her in the hope of winning her favour, lost many years before by his secret marriage to her cousin Lady Catherine Grey. Similarly, when she stayed at Cowdray its owner, Viscount Montague saw it as a good opportunity to prove to her that, although he was a Catholic, his loyalty to her was unimpeachable, and he arranged that while walking through the grounds she should encounter an angler, fishing with nets, who somewhat improbably made a speech which ingeniously linked fishing with treason, saying that 'There be some so muddy-minded that they cannot live in a clear river; as camels will not drink till they have muddied the water with their feet, so they cannot stanch their thirst till they have disturbed the State with their treacheries.' But whether they saw her visit as an opportunity or a burden, whether they were genuinely welcoming or secretly reluctant, people whom Elizabeth chose to visit had no alternative but to put a good face on it and try to please the Queen.

Sometimes that could be difficult. Elizabeth was not an easy guest: not only did she have to be suitably fed, lodged and entertained and given a parting present that she would feel to be generous enough, she was also liable to make exorbitant requests or even to requisition things she liked the look of. At one house it was tactfully recorded that 'to grace his Lordship more, she, of herself, took from him a salt [cellar], and a spoon and fork of fair agate'; at Osterley, the Queen told her host Sir Thomas Gresham that his court-yard was too big and would look much better if it were divided by a wall. Gresham duly fetched workmen from London to work through the night and when Elizabeth got up the next morning she found the wall in place. When she visited Lord Keeper Bacon at his new house at Gorhambury, she left him in no doubt that she did not think it good enough. 'My Lord Keeper,' she said sternly, 'what a little house you have gotten'; as a result, Bacon added to the house a build-ing 120 feet long and eighteen feet wide, with an open loggia on the ground floor and a gallery above it.

A little rebuilding, however, was a minor matter in com-parison with the consequences suffered by some of the Queen's hosts. While she was staying at the house of a Mr. Rookwood at Thetford, a piece of plate went missing and a search was made for it. This unearthed a large image of the Virgin Mary, which was clearly used for Catholic worship. Since Protestant England tolerated the worship of no virgin other than Elizabeth herself, the picture was burnt, and the unfortunate Mr. Rookwood found himself in Norwich jail. He spent the remaining twenty years of his life in prison, with his estates forfeit to the Crown.

This, however, was the exception. Elizabeth's hosts usu-ally suffered nothing worse than depleted finances, and most of the progresses of her reign were markedly successful. Elizabeth could be very gracious when she chose: her godson Sir John Harington said that 'when she smiled, it was pure sunshine that everyone did choose to bask in when they could', and she could also display a ready wit, a robust sense of humour and, when she was touched in the right way, genuine sympathy and kindness. Progresses often brought out the best in her, particularly when she found herself faced with the common people of her kingdom. She knew that she needed to win their hearts, and as her reign wore on she also had increasingly good cause to be grateful to them for the unswerving loyalty and support which they had shown her. Encounters between her and them were almost invariably hugely successful. Once in Huntingdonshire her coach was hailed by a countryman who demanded that it should stop because he wanted to meet the Queen; Elizabeth duly complied, and let him kiss her hand. When the Recorder of Warwick was seen to be shaking visibly throughout his speech to her, Elizabeth reassured him by telling him 'You were not so afraid of me as I was of you.'

In many ways the Queen's progresses in the sixteenth century resembled royal walkabouts and visits to towns in the twentieth. In 1578, when she had been Queen for twenty years, Elizabeth visited Norwich. The city had a history of political and religious troubles, so it was especially important that the Queen's visit should succeed and should effect a reconciliation between the city and the Crown. In fact it was a triumph: Elizabeth showed great interest in pageants representing the cloth-making which was the staple industry of the city—like all good politicians, she paid special attention to the work produced by children, thus pleasing their parents and planting her image in the hearts of those who would grow up to be her subjects—and when her procession missed some people who had been waiting to stage a show for her Elizabeth, hearing of the event, made sure that they were able to perform it for her the next day. When she left she told the citizens 'I have laid up in my head such goodwill as I shall never forget Norwich', and they cried to see her go.

The number of people who thronged to greet her, the terrible state of the roads, the size of the retinue that accompanied her and the discomfort involved in prolonged travel in the unsprung coaches of the sixteenth century meant that going on progress was slow work, especially in the more rural areas. Even in the next century the novelist Daniel Defoe reported that in Sussex the roads were so bad that he had seen a lady going to church in a coach which had to be pulled by six oxen, since horses were unable to move it; and Elizabeth's court on progress was able to move at an average rate of only three miles an hour. This meant that many of her more ambitious plans were never able to be fulfilled. She wanted to go to York, the most important city in the north of the country and the town that had given its name to one of the two royal houses from which she claimed descent, and she also hoped to visit north Wales, ancestral home of the Tudors, but their distance from London meant that she was never able to manage either visit.

On the other hand, there were certain places that she definitely did *not* want to visit: during the nineteen years that her cousin Mary, Queen of Scots, was Elizabeth's prisoner, kept in various houses in the midland and northern counties of England, Mary assiduously pleaded for a chance for the two to meet, and every year the progress route just as resolutely avoided going anywhere where even the question of her being able to meet Mary might arise. There are signs that Elizabeth in some moods might have welcomed the meeting, since it would have provided her with an opportunity to satisfy her curiosity about Mary, but her council were adamantly opposed to it, impressing on her how steadfastly Catholic parts of the north still were and how deep loyalties to local lords and traditions still ran in those parts, in a way that it would take more than one brief progress to change. Partly as a result of this, Elizabeth never went further north than Chartley, in Staffordshire.

In some years the political situation was so unstable that it seemed unwise for her to be out of reach of London, so she would stay in the Home Counties. This was the case in the 1580s, with the years of the execution of Mary, Queen of Scots, and of the Armada, and by the time the various crises were over the courtiers rather hoped that even the seemingly indomitable Elizabeth, now that she was in her late fifties, would tire of going on progresses. Possibly to show that she still could, however, Elizabeth set out on progress again in 1591, and continued to make short progresses even in her last summer. Progresses were too pleasant and too important to be lightly abandoned, because not only did they provide

141

Elizabeth with variety, entertainment and a chance of seeing and being seen by her people outside the capital, they too, like so many other aspects of the Elizabethan age, could be used as vehicles of display to propagate still further the cult of Elizabeth.

This was particularly the theme of the Queen's visits to private houses. Individual cities and the two university towns of Oxford and Cambridge might fête her as Diana, chaste and beautiful goddess of hunting, or as Cynthia, virgin goddess of the moon, or as the Fairy Queen or the Queen of the reborn city of Troy; courtiers, though, were much more intimately acquainted with the specific details of the cult of the Queen and with the ways in which she liked her image to be projected, and they were also anxious to advertise their familiarity with her cult because it showed how close they were to her. A visit by Elizabeth to the house of one of her courtiers provided a golden opportunity for him to display in front of all his fellow courtiers not only the size, magnificence and taste of his house, the ingenuity and fashionableness of his garden, and the splendour of his standard of living, but also how imaginatively, wittily, lavishly and appositely he could entertain his Queen.

One of the most celebrated of all the entertainments offered to Elizabeth on progress was on her visit to Kenilworth in 1575. Kenilworth Castle had, in its day, been one of the most important fortresses in the country; strategically situated in the heart of the Midlands, it had been the stronghold of Simon de Montfort, leader of a rebellion against King Henry III, and after his death had proved its strength by withstanding a famous siege, with the garrison eventually surrendering only because of shortage of food, having been able to force favourable terms. One of the reasons for the castle's strength was that it was surrounded on two sides by a large lake, known as the Mere, which protected it on those two sides and allowed the defenders to concentrate their efforts on the remaining two, which were strongly fortified. After the siege of de Montfort's followers the castle passed to the crown, and as changing patterns of warfare and more peaceful conditions made it less important as a military stronghold, the lake began to be used not only for defence but also for leisure purposes: John of Gaunt built rooms over-looking it, and King Henry V built a pleasure garden, called a 'Pleasaunce', at one end of it, with a little harbour so that small boats could sail out to the garden from the castle. The castle itself also became used less as a fortress and more as a palace; in the fourteenth century John of Gaunt constructed a great hall there that in its day was one of the widest buildings in England.

It remained in the royal family until Elizabeth's brother, King Edward VI, granted it to the powerful John Dudley, Duke of Northumberland, who was scheming to become the effective ruler of England by marrying his son Guildford to Lady Jane Grey and making her Queen of England on Edward VI's imminent death. When his plan failed, Northumberland was executed and his estates forfeited to the crown. His sons were also imprisoned in the Tower; Guildford was executed, but the other sons were eventually released and one of them, Robert Dudley, went on to re-found his family's fortunes by becoming the favourite of Queen Elizabeth. She made him Earl of Leicester, and she also granted him the castle of Kenilworth, so briefly held by his father. Another of Robert's brothers, Ambrose Dudley, was ennobled, being given the title of Earl of Warwick, and received Warwick Castle, close to Kenilworth.

The new Earl of Leicester set about making Kenilworth a castle fit to receive a visit from the Queen and her court. His position as Master of the Horse and favourite of the Queen meant that, even more than most Elizabethans, he was acutely conscious of his status; and Elizabeth was never so absolutely besotted with him that she did not also bestow favours on others, so that Leicester, spurred on by the stimulus of competition, had to make constant efforts to maintain that status. He therefore carried out extensive alterations to the existing castle at Kenilworth to make it into a suitable home for someone who wanted to be taken for the most important nobleman in the land. He built an entirely new block of rooms which were specially designed to house and impress important visitors, being tall, stately, and with huge windows filled with expensive glass, through which expensive candles could glitter ostentatiously at night-time;

he built a new gatehouse on one side of the castle and a new bridge over the Mere on the other, so that from whichever side a visitor approached the first view of the castle would be suitably impressive; he built stables, for the many horses which the Queen and her suite always brought with them; and he redesigned and relaid the garden, filling it, on the model of Henry VIII's garden at Hampton Court, with wooden poles supporting bears holding ragged staffs, the emblem of his house.

All this was ready for the Queen's visit in 1575. She had visited the castle twice previously, but this time she was to make a much longer visit, staying seventeen days in all, and it was Leicester's great opportunity to make an indelible impression. His need to do this was sharpened by the fact that while the Queen was staying at Kenilworth she heard a rumour she did not at all like of a flirtation between Leicester and her own cousin Lettice Knollys, Countess of Essex; the rumour may well have been true—Leicester did eventually marry Lettice after the death of her first husband—and with all the resources of his own home to hand Leicester only just managed to pacify her.

Apart from that one interruption, however, the Queen's stay at Kenilworth was a great success. On the bridge over the Mere were seven pairs of columns hung with gifts for her, in the way offerings were made to a classical goddess. They included plates of fish with fresh grass over them as protection, wheat, grapes and other kinds of fruit, armour hanging from ragged staffs (Leicester's family crest), and two trees hung with harps, lutes, viols, recorders and flutes. When she had crossed the bridge, she found herself greeted by an enormously tall porter standing at the gate and, up above him on the battlements, what appeared to be giants —eight-foot-tall pasteboard figures who appeared to be blowing trumpets, with real trumpeters, blowing a fanfare of welcome, concealed behind them.

The giants were there to allude to the popular stories of King Arthur, in which his knights often encountered giants. The Arthur myth was an enormously popular and powerful one in fifteenth- and sixteenth-century England; legend had it that King Arthur would rise from his enchanted sleep to rule

144

over England in time of need, and Elizabeth's grandfather King Henry VII had taken advantage of his own Welsh birth and of the fact that many stories associated King Arthur with Wales to present himself, and the Tudor dynasty as a whole, as the promised rebirth of Arthurian greatness. He had even called his eldest son Arthur, so that England would indeed have a second King Arthur, but the boy had died young. Elizabeth, too, stressed her Welsh ancestry and presented herself as far as she could in terms of the Arthur myth, and it was to this that Leicester was alluding by having giants on the battlements to welcome her. But the giants had a still further significance: local legend said that Kenilworth Castle itself had been one of King Arthur's castles. This was of course a chronological impossibility—the historical Arthur dated from the sixth century and the castle from the eleventh—but nevertheless it was a pleasing allusion and one which suggested that in coming to the castle of Lord Leicester Elizabeth, the new Arthur, was returning to her true home and that she and her court were entering an enchanted world in which they would find marvels and wonders. To make the point still further, the great clock of the castle was stopped as Elizabeth entered it, and not started again until she left: when she entered Kenilworth, this implied, she was entering a magical, timeless world.

The Arthurian theme was continued when Elizabeth encountered the 'Lady of the Lake'. The Lady of the Lake was a figure who often occurred in the Arthurian cycle: sometimes she was connected with Merlin, or with the boat in which the wounded Arthur was taken away to the Island of Avalon; sometimes she was connected with the mysterious arm clothed in white samite which appeared from the lake to receive the magic sword. Now a woman representing her was borne towards Elizabeth on an artificial floating island, blazing with torches because it was evening and beginning to get dark; she explained to Elizabeth something of the history of the castle. The length of the welcoming ceremonies meant that it was quite dark by the time Elizabeth entered the castle, and she had to wait till next day to see the garden that Leicester had laid out and the splendid aviary he had created built in the form of a classical temple and filled with birds from many countries chosen for the beauty of their plumage and song.

When Elizabeth felt sufficiently rested after her journey to venture outside the castle again, Leicester was careful to provide her with more entertainment. He arranged hunts, bear-baitings, and an Italian acrobat who could twist his body into seemingly impossible shapes; he arranged for Elizabeth to see a local wedding—all the courtiers were much amused by the ugliness of the bride—and afterwards for her to watch some of the local youths taking a turn at the quintain, a sort of joust with a wooden target so contrived that if it was not hit squarely in the centre it would swing round and cover the unfortunate contestant with a large bag of flour. In his anxiety to impress, Leicester had even consulted an Italian fireworks expert on the possibility of putting on a display in which fireworks were attached to live birds, cats and dogs, who were then propelled out of the body of a flying firework dragon (alluding to the Welsh dragon, and to the dragons killed by Arthur and his knights) like living rockets, but fortunately for the cat and dog population of Kenilworth the fireworks expert had decided that it was technically not possible.

Leicester was able, however, to use the Mere to stage a water-pageant. The Lady of the Lake appeared again, accompanied by a triton who explained to Elizabeth that the Lady had been fleeing from the wicked Sir Bruce Sans Pitie when Neptune had provided her temporary refuge by surrounding her with water, thus creating the lake. Merlin had prophesied that she would remain there until she was liberated by 'a better maid than herself', and that had now been happily achieved by the presence of Elizabeth, who was of course the most perfect maid of all. In the same pageant there also appeared an eighteen-foot long mermaid and a floating artificial dolphin bearing on its back a man dressed in a mask who was supposed to represent Arion, the figure from Greek mythology who was saved from drowning by riding on the back of a dolphin, but who was so overawed by the presence of the Queen that after only a few lines of his prepared speech he pulled off his mask and cried out that he was not really Arion at all, but only plain Harry Goldingham.

The Queen almost cried with laughter at this and said it was the best bit of the whole pageant. Some scholars have seen in this the source for Snug the Joiner's similar revelation in Shakespeare's *A Midsummer Night's Dream*: the local people of the Kenilworth area were allowed to watch many of the entertainments put on for the Queen—Leicester was quite happy to display his magnificence to as large an audience as possible—and the young Shakespeare, then aged 11, could well have come with his parents from nearby Stratford to witness this great local event.* He does also refer in *A Midsummer Night's Dream* to 'a mermaid sitting on a dolphin's back', which might be a reminiscence of the Kenilworth water pageant, and it certainly seems true to say that Duke Theseus's tolerant attitude towards the clumsy dramatic attempts of his subjects is very much a parallel to Queen Elizabeth's own patience with the many shows put on for her.

It was perhaps because the pageants in general went down so well that when the one dark spot of the visit arrived, it was with a pageant that Leicester attempted to put it right. Somehow the rumour came to Elizabeth's ears that he was flirting with her cousin Lettice Knollys, Lady Essex, also a guest at the castle, and she wasted no time in showing her displeasure with him. She announced her intention to cut short her trip, stayed in the apartments set aside for her, and refused to watch the prepared pageant of goddesses and nymphs. Leicester therefore ordered the poet George Gascoigne, who had been staying at the castle to write the speeches for the actors, to prepare a special show designed to suit the occasion. When the Queen finally did emerge to go hunting, she was met on the way back by 'Sylvanus', a wild man of the woods, who said he had come to inform her that all the woodland inhabitants of the region were heartbroken to hear that the Queen was thinking of leaving them so soon. His speech was followed by music and by the appearance of a figure who introduced himself as 'Deep Desire' and begged the Queen's forgiveness; he was successful, and the remainder of the visit passed off without a hitch.

* See Elizabeth Jenkins, *Elizabeth and Leicester* (London: Victor Gollancz, 1961; reprinted Granada, 1972), pp 239–42.

Other visits to great country houses worked along similar lines, being designed to offer as many and as ingenious compliments to the Queen as could possibly be squeezed in. When she visited Beddington, the house's owner, Sir Francis Carew, had covered a cherry tree with a tent, to keep the rays of the sun off it and so stop it from ripening until he knew that the Queen's arrival was imminent, when he removed the tent to allow the fruit to ripen, and was able when she arrived to offer his ripe cherries long after the season for them had passed. Even such an apparently simple gesture as this might also have had a secondary meaning alluding to the cult of the Queen: in the mediaeval cherry tree carol, the Virgin Mary wishes for some cherries and the tree bends over at the order of the Christ child to give them to her spontaneously. Perhaps the idea of cherries at command and its association with the Virgin Mary was meant to be present in the minds of those watching this gesture of homage to the Virgin Queen.

Merely retarding the ripening of cherries, however, was as nothing compared with what the Earl of Hertford was prepared to do when Elizabeth announced her intention of visiting his house at Elvetham on her progress of 1591. The Earl had been in disgrace with the Queen since the very earliest years of the reign, when his secret marriage to Lady Catherine Grey had cost him nine years in the Tower. Now he had an opportunity not only to win his way into her good graces but also, perhaps, to obtain from her a favour very close to his heart: he might be able to ask her to recognize the legitimacy of the two sons he had had by Lady Catherine, who were currently declared bastards and so were incapable of inheriting any of his land or property. He was fortunate in that he had very close at hand someone able to advise him exactly how to plan an entertainment for Elizabeth: his second wife Frances Howard, who had once been one of the Maids of Honour and who was still affectionately called by the Queen her 'good Franke'. The Countess of Hertford had had personal experience of progresses in her days as a Maid of Honour, and knew exactly the sort of things that would please Elizabeth best.

First of all there was the question of food. The court

on progress consumed quite phenomenal quantities of food and drink, and Elizabeth was very particular about what was served to her; there had been an alarming occasion at Grafton in 1571 when the Queen had declared that the local ale was too strong for her to drink—she never touched anything stronger than wine mixed with water—and the neighbourhood had had to be scoured for suitable beverages for the thirsty monarch (water alone was considered to be extremely unhealthy and dangerous to the constitution). At nearby Cowdray, where the court was staying before it moved onto Elvetham, three oxen and 140 geese had been eaten at one breakfast alone, while at Gorhambury in 1577, in the time between Saturday evening and the following Wednesday afternoon, the court had eaten eight oxen, sixty sheep, thirty-four lambs, eighteen calves, ten kids, thirty-two stags, twelve dozen herons, thirteen dozen bitterns and lesser numbers of various other species of birds such as godwits, curlews, shovellers, dotterels and knots.

The Countess of Hertford sent out her servants to gather in as much food as they could, and also imported cooks from London to produce the great specialities of Elizabethan banquets, sugar sculptures which were known as 'subtleties'. These were an indispensable part of any Elizabethan entertainment, and they provided yet another opportunity for the giver of a banquet to demonstrate his wit, his ingenuity, and even his loyalty, if he included subtleties in a shape that could be read as containing a compliment to the Queen. The list of the subtleties produced for the visit to Elvetham is particularly impressive, including the arms of the Queen and of all the nobles in sugar-work, and sugar-work men, women, castles, weapons, drummers, trumpeters and soldiers, sugar-work lions, unicorns, bears, horses, camels, bulls, rams, dogs, tigers, elephants, antelopes, dromedaries, apes, eagles, falcons, cranes, bustards, bitterns, pheasants, partridges, quails, larks, sparrows, pigeons, cocks, owls, snakes, adders, vipers, frogs, toads, worms, mermaids, whales, dolphins, sturgeons, conger eels, pikes, carps, breams, and many other fish. It was no wonder the English were famous throughout Europe for their bad teeth.

As well as providing food, the Countess also needed to ensure that there was enough to entertain Elizabeth, and that the entertainment provided was sufficiently splendid. Since the water-pageants at Kenilworth had been such a marked success, the Countess felt that they too should provide a water entertainment. Elvetham did not actually have a lake, but the Countess soon had men at work digging a large-sized pond in the shape of a crescent (a tribute to Elizabeth's association with the virgin moon goddess, variously called Cynthia, Diana, or Belphoebe, whose symbol was the crescent moon) with three islands in it shaped respectively like a ship, a fort, and a snail—the latter being represented by spiralling privet bushes growing up the island, and intended to signify the hideous monster which, in Elizabethan eyes, was Catholic Spain. This was to be the scene for the water pageant.

The Queen was greeted by the Earl himself and 200 followers, all wearing hats decorated with gold chains and black and orange feathers, and by six virgins singing a song of welcome. For the water pageant she was seated beneath a green and silver canopy held up by four knights. The pageant itself consisted of various 'sea gods' (some of them were swimming, but some of them, unfortunately unable to swim, had to make do with wading instead), who made speeches in praise of Elizabeth and presented her with the mandatory gifts. They were followed by a small boat gaily decorated with flags and containing three virgins playing Scottish jigs on cornets—Scottish jigs do not seem particularly appropriate to Elizabeth, but perhaps that was what the three virgins were good at—and then came an interruption by some 'wild men of the woods', who got into a fight with the sea gods which ended, much to the amusement of the spectators, with various of the wild men falling into the water. The battle was taken to represent the war at sea between England and Spain; not surprisingly, the side representing England won.

The Queen's visit to Elvetham was also marked by the great novelty of a game of tennis played not indoors, as was the custom, but outdoors on a lawn, and the celebrations were ended by a dance of 'fairies' on the lawn under the

Queen's window on her last morning there. The fairies sang a song in praise of Elizabeth, which she enjoyed so much that she asked to hear it again. The visit had been a great success, though sadly the Earl of Hertford's attempts to establish the legitimacy of his sons failed miserably; when she heard of it, Elizabeth at once sent him to the Tower, and let him out only after he had paid her a heavy fine which, together with the cost of the Elvetham entertainments, almost ruined him. Progresses and entertainments might be a means of displaying power and status, but no Elizabethan courtier could ever afford for one moment to forget that the power he displayed had been only lent to him by the Queen, and that she could and might choose to strip him of it. However much courtiers might see the entertainments they staged for Elizabeth's visits as vehicles to demonstrate their own magnificence, the structure of the Elizabethan court meant that all such entertainments ultimately revolved around the celebration of the cult of the queen herself and redounded to her greater glory.

VIII

Court Entertainments

ELIZABETH was a hard-working Queen, but she also found time for entertainment. Sometimes this was just sitting gossiping with her ladies, or hunting, which she loved; sometimes it was watching plays, some of them by Shakespeare, which would be specially performed at court; sometimes it was sewing; sometimes it was playing the virginals or dancing, both fashionable accomplishments for women in which Elizabeth was proud of her prowess. Her father King Henry VIII and her grandfather King Henry VII, perhaps because of their Welsh ancestry, had both had a love of music, and Henry VIII had indeed composed songs of his own. Elizabeth had inherited their interest. At Hampton Court she kept a collection of organs, which she was said to know a great deal about, and there was also a perfumed virginal which was all, except for the strings, constructed entirely in glass, and which had on its lid in gold letters a Latin instruction that whoever played it should pray for Elizabeth to live for ever. She also owned a virginal whose strings were made of gold and silver, a set of ivory pipes which imitated the noises made by various animals, and many other instruments, some inherited from her father.

The Queen was said to be a good performer on the virginals, and when she was visited by Sir James Melville, an envoy from her cousin Mary, Queen of Scots, in the period before Mary became Elizabeth's prisoner and was still reigning in Scotland, Elizabeth, with that broad streak of vanity in her which may have been derived from her insecure childhood, was anxious to discover whether she or her cousin were the more accomplished. First of all she asked the unfortunate Melville which was the more beautiful, she or Mary. Melville, torn between not wishing to offend

Elizabeth and wanting to stand up for his own Queen and country, produced the masterly diplomatic reply that Mary was the most beautiful Queen in Scotland, and Elizabeth the most beautiful Queen in England. He was not going to get off so lightly, however. He was next asked which of the two was taller, and he replied immediately and truthfully that Mary, who stood six foot high, was taller than Elizabeth—only to receive the disconcerting reply, 'Then she is too tall for a woman, for I myself am neither too high nor too low.' Next day he found himself being led by Elizabeth's cousin, Lord Hunsdon, to a place where he could secretly hear Elizabeth, alone, performing on the virginals. When she detected his presence she declared that she was angry with him, since she only played for her own enjoyment and never in front of men, but she nevertheless asked him whether she or Mary were the better musician. This time Melville, presumably truthfully, agreed that Elizabeth played better than his own Queen did.

Elizabeth had still another test for him, though. All her life she was immensely fond of dancing, sometimes having her Maids of Honour dance in front of her and very often taking part herself. She even had herself painted while dancing with the Earl of Leicester, in a picture modelled on a French painting of the beautiful Queen Marguerite of Navarre dancing at a ball at the court of France. The final ordeal for Melville was to be invited to watch the Queen dance, and then to tell her whether she or her cousin Mary were the better dancer. Melville's reply is interesting in itself: he told her that his own Queen 'danced not so high or disposedly as she did'. This provides an insight into the high leaps and energetic movements of sixteenth-century dances (one of which, La Volta, was considered so risqué that it was popularly believed to provoke both murders and miscarriages), and it also shows how even dancing could be turned into a means of display. Indeed dancing, like so many other things in Elizabethan England, could even have a symbolic meaning; its ordered, patterned movements always carried with them an undercurrent of representing the harmonious dance of the planets, and sometimes a more specific meaning could be attached to a dance. This became much more the case in the courtly masques of Elizabeth's successors, James I and Charles I, but signs of it were beginning to emerge at the end of her own reign; at one masque eight of her ladies came in as the eight Muses looking for their lost sister, the ninth Muse, who of course was discovered to be the Queen herself. Even a dance could be turned into a compliment to Elizabeth and a contribution to the celebration of her cult.

Another regular and important feature of court life, which also contributed to maintaining the dignity and splendour of the Queen and to impressing those who saw her, was the ceremonial serving of food. This was obviously of the utmost importance at the great formal banquets given on special occasions or to impress important visitors, but the status and power of the Queen were felt to demand that even on ordinary occasions the serving of her food should be performed to the accompaniment of suitable ceremony and ritual. Perhaps because of the symbolic use of bread which is made in the Eucharist, there was a long tradition of displaying one's own status by having one's food treated with reverence; in the kitchen of a great lord it was a punishable offence to turn one's back on the joint of meat which he was going to eat, since this was indicative of disrespect, and when the meat was finally carried into the hall to be eaten, often to the accompaniment of music signalling its arrival, all the retainers had to take their hats off to it. In a similar spirit, the serving of Elizabeth's meals was carried out with impressive ritual.

Two gentlemen would arrive first, one of whom carried a rod, as a sign of his authority, and the other with a table-cloth. Both would advance to the table, kneeling three times on the way, and then spread the tablecloth. They then knelt once more and left. Two more gentlemen followed, kneeling similarly, to put on the table the plate, the bread and the salt cellar (bread and salt were thought of as the staples of life; they had similar symbolic significance until quite recently in some eastern European countries). Next came an unmarried woman wearing white silk, who rubbed the bread and salt over the plate, and a married woman carrying the knife which would be used to 'taste' the food to check whether it was poisoned; they, too, had to kneel the required number

154

of times on entering. When they had finished their duties, they were joined by the Yeomen of the Guard, who had removed their hats as a sign of respect, and who carried in the twenty-four dishes that made up the main course, to the accompaniment of drums and trumpets. Each member of the guard would then receive, from the married woman, a mouthful of one of the dishes, so that any poison concealed in it would show its effects on him before it was given to the Queen.

The length of the ceremony of course meant that the food itself would rapidly be getting cold; but even more astonishingly, all this ceremonial was in fact performed to an empty room. The Queen herself was never there—she found the ceremony tedious and in any case had a very small appetite. She would be waiting in her own apartments, where the Maids of Honour would eventually bring her her choice of dishes from the table, themselves eating what she did not want. The ritual was thus highly impractical, but it did not exist for convenience: it was designed as an indication of the greatness of the Queen. It would have been unthinkable to offer her any less than twenty-four dishes per course, because there was a long tradition that the more important people were, the more they were offered to eat; at mediaeval banquets where pieces of bread, known as trenchers, were used as plates, it was customary for the lowest-ranking people to share their trenchers one amongst four, while the highest-ranking person or people present would have their higher status indicated by being apportioned a trencher for themselves alone.

The sixteenth century, so obsessed with status, had continued the tradition of using food and feasts as a means of display, though nobody could possibly hope to outdo the celebrated dinner parties given earlier in the century by the fabulously wealthy Sienese banker Agostino Chigi. He had once invited the Medici Pope Leo X to a dinner at which every guest was served his food on a plate bearing his personal crest engraved on it; when the Pope complimented him on the dinner and, in particular, on his splendid dining-room, Chigi responded that it was not his dining-room at all but his stable—upon which his servants pulled down the tapestries which had been concealing the rough wooden walls and the rows of feeding-stalls. It was even rumoured that Chigi would order his servants to throw his silver dishes into the Tiber when he had finished eating, to demonstrate that he had so many that he would never need to use them more than once—but, it was said, the same servants would in fact line the river with nets so that they could retrieve the dishes later when they thought no one was looking.

Stories like this, even where they are unfounded, illustrate how in the eyes of the sixteenth century, a public meal in a wealthy household provided another opportunity for the host to impress on all those present his power and wealth. He could even turn the occasion into a display of his ingenuity and wit, if he astonished his guests with elaborate sugar 'subtleties' or with huge pies which, when cut, turned out to contain live birds—or even, in the case of the banquets given by Pope Leo X, live naked children. The status-hungry Elizabethan courtier could not afford to neglect any possible opportunity of boosting his public image.

Another of the forms of entertainment at the Elizabethan court provided similar opportunities for the courtier to display himself in public. This was the tournament, which had been popular throughout the Middle Ages as a means of training knights for battles; exercising them during peace time; giving them a chance to work off aggressions which might otherwise have found an outlet in civil wars and rebellions; and investing the court with an image of chivalry and knighthood. Even when, with the development of new methods and instruments of warfare, the skills nurtured in tournaments began to become increasingly out of date, tournaments themselves remained popular; they could still fulfil the function of imbuing a contemporary court with the aura of Arthurian chivalry, and although the weapons used in them might no longer be up-to-date, they still remained dangerous enough to make the tournament seem a worthy testing-ground to young men anxious to prove themselves. (Mary, Queen of Scots' father-in-law died as a result of injuries sustained in a tournament, and there was great panic when a disguised knight was badly wounded at a tournament at which King Henry VIII was also known to be present in disguise, with the King being forced to unmask to reassure the anxious spectators that it was not he who had been hurt.)

Tournaments, like so many others of the entertainments associated with the courts of the Tudor rulers, had been in high favour at the magnificent court of the Dukes of Bergundy. One of the most celebrated and astonishing of the Burgundian tournaments had been the Tournament of the Golden Tree, held in the market place of Bruges to celebrate the marriage between Charles the Bold (also called Charles the Rash), Duke of Burgundy, and his third wife, Margaret of York, the sister of the English King Edward IV. On this occasion all the legendary wealth and elegance of the Burgundian court, all the chivalric trappings and allegorical spectacle of which it was so fond, were exploited to the full to impress the new Duchess and the ambassadors of her brother King Edward, who, it was hoped, would provide valuable assistance to the Burgundians in their struggle with neighbouring France.

The Duke himself appeared at the tournament in cloth-of-gold encrusted with diamonds, pearls and jewels, wearing in his hat the famous Flanders Ruby, and riding a horse whose caparisons jingled with golden bells. His courtiers and retinue had transformed themselves into the knights, dwarves, giants and ogres of the Arthurian romances, and each contestant as he entered had to hang an illustration of his coat-of-arms on a large golden tree which had been specially put up for the purpose. The tournament was, the spectators were told, being held at the command of the Lady of the Hidden Isle, who had asked that in her honour 100 spears should be broken and 100 sword-cuts received, and that the tree should be covered with the arms of famous champions. Everyone was dressed as elaborately as possible; even the horses wore cloth-of-gold and huge feathered plumes, and one knight entered imprisoned in a black castle on a pageant car, while his attendants carried a large golden key which could be used to release him if the assembled ladies agreed.

The English visitors were suitably impressed; one wrote home to tell his family that nothing had ever been seen like it since the court of King Arthur, and when the celebrations were finally over and the English delegation returned home, the court of King Edward must have heard a great deal about the splendours of the court of the Duke of Burgundy. The new alliance between the two powers meant that they continued to exchange embassies and messages, and soon King Edward had a chance to see for himself how magnificent the court of his brother-in-law was, when a successful rebellion on behalf of his Lancastrian rivals forced him to flee the country for a year and he took refuge in Burgundian lands. Even after the Tudors came to the throne, the link persisted: King Henry VII had spent much of his youth at the court of Brittany, where he would have had the chance to hear a great deal about the wonders of the Burgundian court. He would have seen how much the court culture of Burgundy enhanced the prestige of the duchy, and the lesson would have had a particular relevance for him because his own claim to the throne was such a weak one and consequently needed considerable bolstering. He was in general careful with money, but when he became King of England ceremony was one of the few things on which he did not stint, and although he took no part in them himself, tournaments continued to be a feature of English court life. His son and successor, Elizabeth's father Henry VIII, had also encouraged tournaments, and in the earlier part of his reign had usually jousted in them himself; he had a fine figure and considerable strength, and tournaments provided a welcome opportunity to display this.

Elizabeth herself could not of course take part in tournaments as her father had done, but nevertheless they continued to be a regular feature of court life. They were a particularly suitable form of entertainment for visiting delegations from abroad, when they served a dual purpose: the staging of a tournament in an ambassador's honour was a sign of how important the Queen thought he was and how much she valued his country's friendship, but they also provided a discreet reminder that if a foreign country ever did think of war, then England was full of brave young men who would be able to put up a very good fight indeed. Sometimes, too, a tournament could be made to bear a more specialized meaning: in 1579, when Elizabeth was entertaining the ambassadors from the Duke of Alençon, who wished to marry her, they were shown a masque of Amazons, the fierce warrior women of classical legend, who then fought a series of jousts with some knights. This particular entertainment, with its battle between the sexes, might well have been read as a tactful discouragement of the ambassadors, while it avoided the outright, straightforward answer which Elizabeth so hated.

There was a further dimension to the use of the tournament as a way of signalling to foreign ambassadors England's ability to fight, because Elizabeth could hope that not only might they help to deter foreign powers from contemplating war, they might also prove to be acceptable substitutes for war in the eyes of the young men of her court who were so anxious for military glory. Tournaments might, too, provide a relatively safe and controlled means for channelling off the aggression which men like Essex and Raleigh were likely to display towards anyone whom they saw as their rival for the Queen's favour. Tempers ran high when status and position at court was at stake: the Earl of Oxford had once challenged Sir Philip Sidney to a duel because Sidney was playing tennis on a court which the Earl wanted to use, and on another occasion the Earl of Essex, seeing Sir Charles Blount wearing, tied to his sleeve, a gold chess queen which Elizabeth had given him, had snapped angrily 'Now I perceive that every fool must have a favour.' Blount at once challenged Essex, and succeeded in wounding him in the thigh. That particular affair had in fact ended with the two men becoming fast friends, but duels could not be relied upon always to produce such satisfactory outcomes. At least tournaments usually produced relatively few injuries, and they were fought in public, under the eye of the Queen, so that tempers were likely to be kept under control.

The most important aspect of tournaments, however, was the fact they, like so many features of the Elizabethan court, could be used as a celebration of the cult of Elizabeth. As a woman, the Queen might not be able to joust in them as her father had done, but tournaments had traditionally been presided over by a woman: the most beautiful lady present was appointed Queen of the Tournament and would distribute the prizes. This was a rôle admirably suited for Elizabeth to play, since it made her the central figure of the tournament and also cast her in the rôle of most beautiful woman present; it made her into a romantic heroine, and transformed her courtiers into paladins of chivalry, fighting for her. Some years after the beginning of the reign, the Queen's rôle was expanded still further when her Champion Sir Henry Lee declared that every year for so long as he was able he would present himself armed in the Tiltyard on the anniversary of the Queen's accession, 17 November, to take on all comers. Soon the Accession Day tilts had become a yearly celebration of Elizabeth's reign, interrupted only in 1582 when the court could not come to London because the plague was raging so fiercely there.

In the case of the Accession Day Tilts one can see with particular clarity how Elizabeth deliberately set about creating celebrations in her own honour that would replace, and compensate for the loss of, those of the Catholic church. Explicit references are made in speeches and sermons to the fact: at one tilt a knight arrived with some men from the country and explained that they had been told by their curate that this was a day that was better than 'all the pope's holidays'; at another Sir Philip Sidney's retinue spoke a poem referring to the day as a 'sabbath' and Elizabeth herself as its presiding saint. Coincidentally, 17 November was only two days before St. Elizabeth's Day, 19 November, and celebrations would often spread to cover St. Elizabeth's Day as well—only now, of course, it was no longer St. Elizabeth who was being celebrated, but Queen Elizabeth. Just as the Christian church had once taken over pagan festivals, choosing to celebrate the day of Christ's birth on 25 December, the day once sacred to the Festival of the Unconquered Sun, so Elizabeth appropriated to her own use the holy days of the Catholic church.

The importance of the occasion meant that her courtiers did their best to put on as splendid a show as possible. Those who could afford it would have one or more suits of richly decorated and often symbolic armour: the Earl of Cumberland had one set covered with stars, and another set with Tudor roses, fleurs-de-lys as a sign of the traditional

English claim to the throne of France, and 'E's for Elizabeth. Armour was expensive, and courtiers were often so proud of it and of the chivalric rôle it represented that they had their pictures painted in it. Such portraits also often feature the *impresa* motto of the knight. The *impresa* was the device borne on the knight's shield. Normally the shield would show the coat-of-arms of its wearer; but for tournaments a different convention was adopted, whereby each knight was expected to display on his shield a picture and an accompanying motto, usually either witty or containing an elaborate compliment to the Queen, or sometimes conveying a message to her. Since the shields were all given to the Queen and were eventually displayed in the Shield Gallery at Whitehall, considerable care, ingenuity and invention was invested in them; in the reign of Elizabeth's successor the Earl of Rutland, obviously feeling he was not up to producing a suitable *impresa* by himself, commissioned Shakespeare to make him one. Usually, however, it was a matter of honour to devise your own, and to express as much ingenuity as possible in its construction.

Sometimes *imprese* could contain heraldic references. The Dudley ragged staff was a particularly suitable shape, and so too was the Howard crest of a white lion; at one tilt a certain Mr. Coningsby, who was unsuccessfully in love with the Queen's Maid of Honour Frances Howard, appeared bearing a shield showing a rabbit (often called a coney, and thus a pun on his own name, Coningsby) being eaten alive by a white lion, with the motto 'Call you this love?' Occasionally the message was instantly clear, as in the shield borne on one occasion by the Earl of Essex, which bore no picture at all but only a Latin motto which translated as 'Nothing can represent his sorrow', and which may have been carried by Essex either after the Queen had learned of his secret marriage to Frances Walsingham or some years earlier, as an expression of grief for his friend Sir Philip Sidney.

At other times the allusions could be more obscure, demonstrating the wit and learning of the shield's bearer. One carried in the very early years of the reign by Robert Dudley, later to be created Earl of Leicester, showed a pyramid surrounded by ivy: ivy was a sign of fidelity, and the pyramid, being a symbol of the Virgin Mary in her rôle as Divine Wisdom, was a suitable way of representing Elizabeth, so that the whole together would mean that Dudley was supported by the wisdom of Elizabeth, to which he would be always faithful. The meaning was underlined by the Latin motto, which, translated, meant 'While you stand, I shall flourish.' Another shield showed a unicorn dipping his horn in a stream, with the message, again in Latin, that 'I banish poisons'; unicorn's horns were popularly believed to counteract the effects of poisons, and the image as a whole could be a compliment to the Queen, who used a unicorn as one of her heraldic supporters and could be seen as purifying wherever she came, or could refer to the bearer himself, who might perhaps be a courtier who felt himself to have a rival and could be declaring that his is a wholesome influence which could rid the Queen of the noxious presence of his rival. Part of the delight felt by the Elizabethans in the *impresa* arose from just such ambiguity, because it meant that not only the bearer of the shield but also the audience, too, were able to display ingenuity, he by devising the shield and they by decoding it.

Sometimes a knight might use, in successive years, a sequence of related *imprese* which, taken together, told a story. Sir Philip Sidney initially used the motto 'Spero', the Latin for 'I hope', to indicate his optimism about his abilities and prospects; but after he had suffered a serious disappointment, he appeared at a tournament bearing as his *impresa* the word 'Speravi' (Latin for 'I have hoped') crossed out. It is suggested that this may refer to an occasion when he appeared at a tournament immediately after his uncle, the Earl of Leicester, had had a son, an event which had spoiled Sidney's chances of succeeding his uncle in the earldom; or he may have used the 'Speravi' device after he had annoyed the Queen by writing her a letter trying to dissuade her from marrying the Duke of Alençon; it would certainly fit in with the fact that for his New Year's gift to her that year he had given her a jewelled whip, representing his recognition of her right to command him.

Earlier in the reign, at the Accession Day Tilt in 1577, Sidney appeared as the Shepherd Knight, Philisides. This

162

was clearly a play on his own name, and it could also be taken as meaning 'lover of a star': 'Stella', the Latin word for star, was the name he gave in his poetry to Penelope Devereux, sister of the Earl of Essex, whom Sidney loved but who was forcibly married to another man whom she detested. The title of 'The Shepherd Knight' placed Sidney within the pastoral world of romance, which was so dear to the Elizabethans and which he wrote about in his own 'The Countess of Pembroke's Arcadia'; it lent him an air of simple truthfulness and incorruptibility, and perhaps he felt it to suit the fact that although his mother's family were wealthy and important—a fact of which he was very proud—his father was in such straitened financial circumstances that he had to decline a peerage because he felt unable to support the associated standard of living. Sidney himself was hoping for a position at court which would advance his fortunes, and his *impresa* showed a tree which was half alive and half dying—signifying that he still hoped that Elizabeth might give him a post, but was at present suffering for the want of one. His lances were made of wild poles and his armour was covered in bark and moss; the poles could be read as an allusion to the ragged staff badge of the Dudley family, to which his mother belonged, and the armour as a reference to the fact that his father was at the time Lord Deputy in Ireland (Philisides claimed to come from 'desert lands', and Ireland was very desert indeed in the eyes of the Elizabethans).

The rustic image was underlined by the fact that Sidney's arrival was heralded by country music and he was accompanied by a group of ploughmen—probably Sidney servants in costume—one of whom spoke a poem explaining that Philisides had obtained permission to celebrate this 'sabbath' day. Sidney appears to have been consummately successful in creating for himself a striking and appropriate image, because 'Philisides' became the name by which many people wrote and spoke of him in the tributes to him written after his death.

Sidney was not the only person to devise a dramatic entrance for himself. In 1581 the Earl of Oxford, a hot-tempered and rather vicious young man who was intensely proud of his ancestry and position, appeared as the Knight of the Tree of the Sun. He pitched for himself a large tent of orange-tawny taffeta, decorated with silver, and waited in his tent until everyone else had arrived, when he emerged to sit down underneath a gilded bay-tree, representing the Tree of the Sun itself, which he had had placed ready for him. A speech made to the Queen by the Earl's page explained the significance of the tree: being unique, it represented Elizabeth herself, who like the phoenix was the only one of her kind. It was also, the Queen was informed, the nesting place of the bird of the virgin Roman goddess Vesta; Cupid had tried several times to shoot his arrow at the bird, but had always had to give up the attempt because he had been blinded by her beauty. The tree thus became the focus of a series of compliments to Elizabeth. The tent was a practical touch, since it would keep the sun off him and prevent him from being over-heated in his armour, but it would also have been read as a reference to the pavilions frequented by the knights of the Arthur stories.

A pavilion was also used when, at the end of the Accession Day Tilt of 1590, Sir Henry Lee, the Queen's Champion, decided that the time had finally come to make use of the let-out clause he had allowed himself when he had promised, many years before, to fight for the Queen's honour every year for as long as death or infirmity did not prevent him. He was 57 now, elderly in Elizabethan terms, and he wanted to retire to live out his days in peace at his country house of Ditchley in Oxfordshire, so he combined his request to be allowed to retire with a final pageant to crown his career as Queen's Champion. He appeared wearing over his armour a surcoat embroidered with vines, signifying that he himself was a vine who had been withered by age. Then the earth appeared to open to produce a white taffeta pavilion designed in the same way as the temple of the Vestal Virgins was supposed to have been—a reference to Elizabeth, who was sometimes shown in her portraits as a vestal virgin. Within the pavilion were an altar with lights burning upon it—another indication of the way in which the cult of Elizabeth had acquired quasi-religious significance—and what was sure to please the Queen, presents, which were handed to her by three 'vestal maidens' while a song set to music by John Dowland was sung, which expressed Sir Henry's desire to retire to the country, use his tilting helmet as 'a hive for bees' and spend his time praying for his 'saint'. Beside the pavilion stood a crowned pillar—a pillar was another symbol often used by Elizabeth, adapted from the device showing the Pillars of Hercules used by the Emperor Charles V—which had winding round it an eglantine tree, eglantine being the rose especially associated with Elizabeth. Pinned to the pillar was a poem in praise of the Queen.

Lee's pageant was a success, and he was allowed to leave the court, his place as Queen's Champion being taken by the Earl of Cumberland, who appeared under the suitably Arthurian-sounding title of the Knight of Pendragon Castle. Arthur's father had been called Uther Pendragon, and it so happened that one of the Earl's actual castles was called Pendragon, so he appeared on this occasion on a pageant car representing the castle, accompanied by a man representing Merlin who made Elizabeth a long and complicated speech about a castle which had been completed only when two dragons, one red and one white, had been persuaded to stop fighting; the colours of the dragons clearly referred to the Wars of the Roses, and dragons were both associated with Arthurian legend and were also the badge of Wales, as well as being appropriate to the name of the castle. Cumberland was also wearing a white surcoat to honour the Virgin Queen, white being the colour of virginity. Another knight appeared at the same tilt in white and green, which together were the traditional colours of the Tudors, and Ferdinando Stanley, Lord Strange, came with thirty-odd squires and a pageant car in the shape of a ship, on which was a model of the Stanley crest, an eagle, which could be made to bow to the Queen.

Cumberland was not the obvious choice as Lee's successor. The outstanding figure at the Tilts since the death of Sidney had undoubtedly been the Earl of Essex, but unfortunately for Essex the year of Lee's retirement coincided with a period of disgrace for him after the Queen had learned of his marriage to Frances Walsingham, Sidney's widow. Instead of appearing at the 1590 Accession Day Tilt as the

165

Queen's new Champion, therefore, Essex entered instead with his friend Sir Fulke Greville dressed entirely in black and sitting in a coal-black chariot drawn by black horses and driven by a figure representing Father Time. The black obviously represented his sorrow at having displeased the Queen, but he was also able to turn it into a compliment to her by having his page dressed in black and white, the personal colours of Elizabeth. Essex was not the only person to try to use a tournament to win back the Queen's favour; Sir Robert Carey, another courtier who had displeased her by marrying, appeared at one tilt in the guise of the Unknown and forsaken knight, who had sworn to live alone, as a hermit, whom nothing but the sight of the Queen could have persuaded to break his vow. Carey was taking no chances, however; in case the Queen did not prove susceptible to allegorical compliments on this occasion, he also presented her with a very expensive gift.

Tournaments were not held only for the Queen's Accession Day. In April 1581 the Earl of Arundel, Lord Windsor, Sir Philip Sidney, and Sidney's faithful follower Sir Fulke Greville (who, at the end of his very long life, had on his tomb the words 'Friend to Sir Philip Sidney') issued a challenge in the name of the Four Foster Children of Desire. The bearer of their challenge was a boy wearing red and white, the colours of desire and also the colours of the Tudor rose, who was sent to the Queen to tell her that the Four Foster Children desired her so much that if she did not immediately yield herself to them, then they would besiege her, and defied all the knights of her court to defeat them. This was in fact an elaborate way of announcing a forthcoming tournament. When it was staged, the next month, Elizabeth was cast as Beauty and the gallery in which she sat became the Fortress of Beauty, the object of the Four Foster Children's siege. They did not, however, succeed in capturing it; the knights of Elizabeth's court defended her in true romance style, and Beauty remained serenely safe in her fortress.

On one level, the tournament held by the Four Foster Children of Desire was merely an elaborate compliment to the Queen: it cast her in the rôles of an Arthurian heroine and of the personification of beauty. It also, however, contained a deeper message. This was the period when Elizabeth did appear to be seriously considering marriage with the Duke of Alençon, and a marriage to a Catholic French duke was something to which Sidney, who saw himself as the champion of the Protestant cause, and his friends were adamantly opposed. The tilt could function as a tactful way of reminding the Queen that in an ideal world, the Fortress of Beauty remained impregnable and Beauty herself remained untouched by desire. At one point during the two-day tournament two knights had actually entered in armour covered with apples and fruit; one of them represented Adam, and the other, who had false hair attached to his helmet, was Eve, and the implication of the little drama they enacted was that for Elizabeth to marry Alençon would be the equivalent of a second fall. Normally Elizabeth bitterly resented any advice offered on the subject of her possible marriage, but on this occasion the tournament was so flattering to her that it was impossible to react ungraciously.

But although Sidney and his friends had succeeded on this occasion in using a tilt to make their point, the game they were playing was a dangerous one. The Queen might have been so flattered by the Four Foster Children of Desire's extravagant compliments to her that she was prepared to overlook the impertinence of their daring to offer her advice, but in general she took it very poorly when her courtiers tried to stage their tournament entrances and pageants round themselves rather than her. This was clearly illustrated at the Accession Day Tilt in 1575, when the Earl of Essex produced an immensely long and enormously expensive entertainment which he appears to have scripted himself, and which centred on the two characters of Erophilus (which in Greek meant 'lover of love') and Philautia, another Greek name which translates as 'lover of self'.

The pageant which was enacted round these two figures took far longer than was customary for a tournament, holding up all the other knights who were waiting to make their entrances, and it also contained many references to previous pageants and entertainments provided for the Queen, mainly by the Cecil family. Although William Cecil, Lord

Burghley, had been Essex's guardian in his youth, Essex now felt that Burghley and his son, Robert Cecil, were his enemies. He resented the amount of dependence Elizabeth placed on their advice, and he had recently had a particularly bitter feud with them when he had tried unsuccessfully to get his friend and protégé Francis Bacon two successive jobs, both of which had gone to Cecil nominees. In the 1595 tournament, therefore, Essex introduced other elements which seem to have been intended as satires on the Cecils and on the entertainments they themselves had provided for the Queen on some of the numerous occasions when she had visited Burghley at his house of Theobalds.

In view of Elizabeth's continued support of the Cecils, this was probably rash enough, but even more unwise was the fact that Essex in this pageant presented himself as having to choose between the rôle of Erophilus, who loved the Queen, and Philautia, who represented self-love, probably in the sense of ambition or of attending to one's own interests. He did of course end by deciding to choose Erophilus, but the way in which he presented the choice could hardly have been satisfactory in the eyes of the Queen. He had suggested that in deciding to devote himself to her he was making a sacrifice of his own interests; this was contrary to the image of the Queen as a mistress whom everybody voluntarily adored, and it also presented her as a ruler who was niggardly with rewards. It might be the truth, but it was still not tactful to say so to Elizabeth at a tournament in her honour. It was even insulting of Essex to represent himself as having to make a choice between his own interests and those of the Queen; for any loyal subject, and certainly for any courtier who claimed to adore her, the question of such a choice should not even arise. Any true lover would automatically put the interests of his mistress before his own, and would indeed regard the interests of his mistress as being the same as his own. Elizabeth was not impressed by Essex's pageant, and she did not hesitate to show her displeasure. She left the tournament without saying anything other than that if she had thought she would have been the subject of so much comment, she would not have bothered to come.

168

In putting on a pageant which cast himself and not Elizabeth as the central character, Essex had committed the cardinal sin of the Elizabethan court: he had forgotten that all its members and all its ceremonies existed solely for the greater glory of the sovereign. Elizabeth might like her courtiers handsome and splendid and her Maids of Honour pretty, but neither group must ever forget that they were supporting players in a drama of which she was the heroine, that they were stars in the presence of the sun. The offence of Essex in using a court entertainment for his own glory rather than that of the Queen had been the same as that of Lucifer, once the brightest angel in the court of heaven but now, through pride, through a reluctance to accord the proper praises to the divinity, fallen to the depths of Hell. Both had attempted to rise above their proper position; both were punished for it. For Elizabeth too, for her own court, was a kind of goddess, and the Accession Day Tilts, like the other entertainments of her court, were a part of her ritual.

Elizabeth in Art and Literature

THE various rôles associated with the Queen, such as Diana, Cynthia, Belphoebe, the Rose of Beauty, the Saviour of the Protestant church, the Vestal Virgin and even the Virgin Mary, filtered through into depictions of her in art and literature. One important feature of most Italian Renaissance courts had been the discovery by their rulers that artists and writers could be used as important tools in the promotion of their image. The Medici rulers of Florence had pointed the way in this; they had founded an academy of writers and thinkers, and they had brought up artists like Michelangelo in their own house alongside the Medici children, partly from a genuine interest in art and learning but also in the hope that their public image as rulers of Florence would be enhanced by such patronage and by the works of art and literature that resulted from it.

Other Italian rulers began to follow suit, and those who did not paid the penalty for it. When Rodrigo Borgia was elected Pope Alexander VI, he took no interest in patronizing scholars and writers, and consequently found himself on the receiving end of a very bad press indeed from them. In many ways the behaviour of the Borgias was no worse than that of members of the Medici family; but the Medici cultivated their image, and were lauded as patrons of the arts, while the Borgias neglected theirs and so acquired a reputation as monsters without parallel.

Poems in praise of Elizabeth were a common feature of entertainments at tournaments and on progresses, and they also appeared in other contexts. In 1600 the poet John Davies published a book of poems entitled *Hymns to Astraea*. Astraea was a figure mentioned in the *Eclogues* of the Roman poet Virgil; she was a Just Virgin who had ascended to Heaven, and when she came back to earth her return would herald the arrival of a new Golden Age. The myth has obvious parallels with both the legend of the return of King Arthur, which was so strongly associated with the Tudor dynasty, and also, in its mention of a virgin who ascends to heaven, with the accounts of the Assumption of the Virgin Mary (although a pagan poet, Virgil was accorded a special status by sixteenth-century humanists because a passage in his work was taken as referring to the coming of Christ). Astraea therefore became another of the symbolic personae associated with Elizabeth, and Davies' book contained twenty-six poems in her honour, all of them in the form, so dear to the Elizabethan mind, of acrostics, so that the initial letters of each line of each poem spelt out the words 'Elisabetha Regina,' as in the following example:

TO FLORA

Empress of flowers, tell where away
Lies your sweet court this merry May
In **Greenwich** garden allies?
Since there the heavenly powers do play
And haunt no other vallies.

Beautie, virtue, majesty,
Eloquent Muses, three times three,
The new fresh **Hours** and Graces,
Have pleasure in this place to be,
Above all other places.

Roses and lilies did them draw,
Ere they divine **Astraea** saw;
Gay flowers they sought for pleasure;
Instead of gathering crowns of flowers,
Now gather they Astraea's dowers,
And bear to heaven their treasure.

Elizabeth herself was fond of reading and also enjoyed watching plays. The legend that she enjoyed the character of Sir John Falstaff, in Shakespeare's *Henry IV* and *Henry V* plays, so much that she asked the playwright to show Falstaff in love and was thus responsible for *The Merry*

Wives of Windsor, cannot be proved, though it is not improbable; but she certainly had plays, including Shakespeare's, frequently performed at court. She was less keen, though, on *Gorboduc,* a play which showed the catastrophes brought about in a kingdom that was left without a universally recognized successor.

The most famous and elaborate evocation of Elizabeth in literature, however, was in *The Faerie Queene.* Its author, Edmund Spenser, came from Ireland, where he was introduced to Sir Walter Raleigh, one of the Queen's favourites. Raleigh persuaded Spenser to come to England with him and use his poetic talents to make his fortune. The promised fortune never materialized (Spenser bitterly lamented the fact that while Elizabeth was full of admiration for his work, she was by no means eager to give him any financial reward for it), and the projected twelve books of *The Faerie Queene* were never completed, but the six books that were written provide considerable insight into the complex of chivalric, romantic, allegorical, heraldic and emblematic influences in which Elizabethan court culture was steeped. It is peopled with wandering knights, personifications, and characters from romances alongside thinly disguised versions of Spenser's own contemporaries: Mary, Queen of Scots, appears in it as Duessa, the double-tongued, dissimulating enchantress, while Elizabeth herself is represented by both the chaste huntress Belphoebe and by the Faerie Queene herself, who is being sought by King Arthur. *The Faerie Queene,* like Sir Philip Sidney's great work *The Countess of Pembroke's Arcadia,* grew out of the court culture of Elizabeth, and reflects its origins.

If literature could reflect court life, the image of the Queen herself could be most directly and powerfully conveyed by pictures of her. Art had been used by all the Tudor rulers as a way of expressing their power and publicizing their image. When Elizabeth's grandfather King Henry VII had contemplated acquiring a new wife for himself and healing his long quarrel with Burgundy (where the late Duchess had been a sister of King Richard III, whom Henry had killed) by marrying the young and beautiful Margaret of Austria, a daughter of the ducal house of Burgundy, he had attempted to make himself more palatable to her by importing a painter from her native, Burgundian-ruled Flanders to produce a portrait of him in the fashionable Flemish style, showing only his head, shoulders and hands. The idea that lay behind this was that a portrait in such a style would make Henry seem more fashionable and sophisticated, rather than the parvenu king which he really was, and that England would appear less of an uncultured backwater and more a place where a daughter of the ducal house of Burgundy could contemplate going to live. In the event Margaret of Austria decided that she would remain a widow, as a token of her love for her dead husband, but the idea of using the portrait as a means of expressing regal power and authority remained.

Although the message of the royal portrait remained the same—the power, status, and magnificence of the sitter— the style in which these attributes were expressed changed. Elizabeth's father, King Henry VIII, had had his own image most perfectly captured in a painting by Holbein, which had become the model for many copies by other artists. The king was no longer shown head and shoulders, as his father had been; Henry VIII was proud of his powerful body, which in his earlier years at least was strong and athletic, and the portraits show him full length. Sometimes, as in the version at Parham Park in Sussex, he is shown standing with feet firmly and confidently planted on a Turkish carpet, a sign of his wealth (Turkish carpets were so expensive that they were normally not walked on at all, but used only on tables, where they would suffer less wear). He stands at a very slight angle, so that his elegant calves can be shown, but his body is shown almost foursquare so that its size can be fully appreciated. The breadth of his shoulders is further increased by the fur-trimmed shoulders of his garment; he looks as though he could wrestle an ox to the ground. His doublet is richly embroidered, his fur is the expensive ermine, worn only by the high-ranking, and he wears jewels on his fingers, in his hat and round his neck. His codpiece is also prominent. His features are set and resolute. It is a striking image of authority.

If Henry VIII's are some of the most impressive of royal portraits, then the saddest is the portrait of his son, King

173

Edward VI, executed by an unknown artist and now in the National Portrait Gallery. Edward, a boy of ten or so, is shown standing in the same pose as his father, dressed in very much the same style; but the difference is striking. Instead of jutting solidly out, his shoulders slope away; his legs have almost no calf at all; the codpiece is barely visible, and the features look childish and rather frightened. There are even fewer jewels. All the portrait suggests is Edward's inadequacy to play the rôle of his dead father.

The portrait of Edward VI serves as an illustration of some of the problems which began to bedevil the portrayal of the monarch after the death of Henry VIII. In Henry VIII's case, his own body had provided a sufficiently splendid image to function as the focal point of the painting, and to imbue it with majesty and authority; in the case of his three children, Edward, Mary and Elizabeth, this was no longer so. Furthermore, there was no native English tradition of portrait painting to speak of, and the isolation of England from the continent brought about by Henry VIII's Reformation of the Church meant that England rapidly began to lose touch with foreign artists and with new developments in the world of art. By the time of Elizabeth I it had become very much an artistic backwater. The greatest native English artist, Nicholas Hilliard, was able to reach heights of genius in some of his miniatures of head and shoulders, but he was weak on perspective and his full-length portraits were very much less successful.

What made the position more difficult was that Elizabeth was torn between two contradictory desires: Hilliard might be deficient in certain areas of technique, and his work might command no respect outside England, but in many ways the sort of image he produced was the one that best suited her. Hilliard painted her flat and frontally lit, without shadow, and these were characteristics that had been associated with the styles of early medieval artists and also of artists of courts like that of Byzantium, and these styles had been used mainly for the portrayal of saints and of the Virgin. As a result such styles had become inextricably associated with the portrayal of holy things; and this was a fact that suited Elizabeth very well indeed, since it invested her portraits

174

with an added dignity and resonance and elevated their status. By contrast, if paintings of her included shadow, as Italian portraits did, it made her look less elevated and indeed reduced her to the level of everybody else, making her appear subject to the normal conditions of light and shade rather than serenely and ethereally remote from them.

As a result, Elizabeth's few encounters with foreign artists were not, on the whole, successful. They might be technically better than Hilliard and other English painters like George Gower; but their style suited her less well. So although the French-trained Isaac Oliver, a painter of considerable skill, was actually living in England for the later part of Elizabeth's reign, Elizabeth sat for him only once and disliked the result, and when the Flemish Marcus Gheeraerts painted the so-called 'Ditchley' portrait of her, now in the National Gallery, she must have expressed similar reservations, because all the later copies based on the Ditchley portrait show the Queen's features as much softer and smoother than they are in the original. The way in which her features were depicted was something that Elizabeth was becoming more and more sensitive about as she advanced into old age, and she even went so far as to order the destruction of all portraits of her that were to her 'great offence'; this move may perhaps have been prompted by the insufficiently flattering portrait produced by Oliver, whose foreign training led him to produce an image of her that looked too little like the goddess of court myth and too much like a gaunt, ageing and all too human woman, who was subject like other humans to the passing of time and to mortality.

The visit earlier in the reign of the Italian artist Federigo Zuccaro, however, was rather more successful, for it seems to have been Zuccaro who introduced Elizabeth to an element of portrait-painting which was to play a very important part in the development of her painted image: the full-scale use of allegory. Previous portraits of Elizabeth, like those of her sister Mary, had suffered in their attempts to produce a suitably splendid image of the Queen from the fact that she was a woman. This meant that she could not be portrayed in armour, or standing with her legs wide apart, traditional techniques for suggesting the might and authority of the sitter; but now Zuccaro brought it to the Queen's attention that allegory could be used instead to suggest her importance and her noble qualities. Allegory had been used before in portraits of Elizabeth, but never on such a scale, so this was a major step forward in the development of portraits of Elizabeth. Pictures of the Queen ceased to look like pictures of a richly-dressed woman and became symbolic depictions of an embodiment of wisdom, virtue and power.

There were many symbols and emblems used in the portraits of Elizabeth. In his original sketch of her Zuccaro had included an ermine, a dog and a pillar with a snake coiled around it. The ermine stood for purity, because it was believed that if an ermine was being hunted and it came across a patch of muddy ground, then it would stop its flight, and allow itself to be caught and killed rather than run on and so get mud on its fur. It was therefore a symbol of resolute virgins who would rather be killed than lose their chastity. The dog stood for faithfulness, since dogs were supposed always to be faithful to their masters, the serpent was a sign of wisdom, and the column can probably be read as a reference to the Pillars of Hercules, a device adopted by the Emperor Charles V, ruler of Spain. The Pillars of Hercules had represented the limits of the known world in classical times, but now a new world, America, had been discovered, and the Emperor Charles laid claim to it, so he therefore used as his device a representation of the Pillars of Hercules with a Latin motto indicating that there was land beyond them. It had always rankled with Elizabeth's father Henry VIII that Charles, his enemy, could claim the title of Emperor while he himself was only a king, and the mythmakers of the Tudor court had accordingly set about claiming that in fact England herself ought to count as an empire. They produced stories of King Arthur being crowned as an Emperor and of continental kings doing him service as such; and the Elizabethan magician John Dee even declared that America had not in fact been first discovered by the Spanish protégé Christopher Columbus but by an eleventh-century Welsh prince, Madoc, who was, he said, a distant ancestor of Queen Elizabeth, and that consequently it was England, not Spain, to whom the

New World rightfully belonged. The use of the pillar device by Elizabeth was another aspect of her claim to be as good as the Emperors themselves.

Later paintings of the Queen adopted some of these symbols introduced by Zuccaro and also added others of their own. The Queen was painted wearing jewels in the shape of a pelican and of a phoenix; the phoenix rose again from its own ashes without reproduction, so was a reassuring symbol that the succession would be made certain without Elizabeth having to marry, and the pelican was a symbol of Christ because it was believed to feed its young on its own blood just as Christ gave his own blood for the communion service, so that the implication was that Elizabeth, too, was the saviour and nourisher of her people. In other paintings she was shown holding a sieve; in Roman legend, a vestal virgin accused of unchastity had proved the falseness of the allegation by carrying water in a sieve without losing a single drop of it, so the sieve in pictures of Elizabeth functions as a compliment to her chastity. Her virginity, which had once been a political liability, can here be seen being transformed into a vital part of her image, and it is also referred to in the portrait of her with an ermine, wearing a collar in the shape of a crown around its neck, sitting on her sleeve.

Several portraits included imperial pillars or columns; some went further still, and, like the 'Armada' portrait, painted to celebrate England's defeat of the Spanish, showed the Queen with her hand resting on a terrestrial globe, to show her dominion over it. In the same painting she is also shown with a closed crown—that is, not an open circlet but a crown with a little velvet cap and two crossed bands of gold covering it. This was the style of crown traditionally worn by emperors, and so functions as another indication of England's claim to a status equal to that of the Holy Roman Emperors. In other paintings of her, Elizabeth is shown with her symbol of the moon, either in the shape of a jewel in her hair or embroidered on the bodice of her dress: as well as being a symbol of her chastity, since the classical goddess of the moon was also the goddess of virginity, the moon governed the movement of the tides and so represented Elizabeth's control over the seas, which was seen by the

177

English as culminating in their defeat of the Armada.

In one painting, the 'Ditchley' portrait, she is shown standing on a map of England, with her feet on Oxfordshire, a reference to the fact that Sir Henry Lee, her former champion, who had commissioned the painting, lived at Ditchley in Oxfordshire. The Ditchley portrait dates from late in the reign, and in it the imagery of Elizabeth has become even more elaborate: it shows a storm in the background on one side of the painting and clear sky on the other, suggesting that Elizabeth now has power not only to rule the earth and the seas but to control the weather as well. Other late portraits of her include one in which she is shown under a triumphal canopy in a way associated with Roman heroes, and the great 'Rainbow' portrait. In this Elizabeth holds a rainbow, which is the symbol of peace; it was a rainbow that God put in the sky after the Flood as a sign of his covenant with Noah and his descendants. She is also wearing a cloak embroidered with eyes and ears to show her constant awareness and alertness, and on her sleeve is an embroidered serpent, symbol of wisdom. Other aspects of her costume also have allegorical and emblematic significance, but the most striking thing of all about the portrait is the face. This picture was painted in 1600, when Elizabeth was 66 years old; yet it shows a young and beautiful woman without a trace of a line or wrinkle.

In her last years, Elizabeth had found that more than allegory was needed to produce the right image of her in paintings. As she aged, and as people's minds turned more and more to the question of her possible successor, the courtly cult of the Queen produced ever more extravagant references to her continuing, eternal youth and beauty. Elizabeth no longer sat for her portraits; all paintings of her of which she did not approve were destroyed, and her painters were issued with a standard version of her head and face which was to form the basis for all future portraits. This standard version was almost certainly produced by Nicholas Hilliard, and it showed the Queen with the long, flowing hair of a virgin, smooth skin, and soft, regular features. Hilliard even produced a new portrait of the Queen at her coronation, although it was now forty-two years after the original event.

Nothing must be left unattempted in the struggle to preserve the fading magic of Elizabeth.

But no art can defeat time. By the end of the year 1602 it was obvious that the Queen was failing, and that the Elizabethan era was drawing to a close. She talked a lot about Essex, and she fell into a melancholy from which nothing could rouse her; her witty godson Sir John Harington attempted to amuse her, but Elizabeth said to him, 'When thou dost feel creeping time at thy gate, these fooleries will please thee less; I am past my relish for such matters.' Finally, in March 1603, at her palace of Richmond, Elizabeth faced death. For some days she had been eating and drinking almost nothing, and spending her time sitting in a low chair. Eventually she tried to get up from it, and found that she could not. Her attendants had to help her up. She had not the strength to walk; but she knew that if she sat down she could never get up again. So, indomitable to the last, the old Queen simply stood where she was, quite rigid, and ignoring all the pleas of her attendants, for fifteen hours.

Finally her strength failed her. But she still refused to go to bed; she made her attendants place cushions for her on the floor, and lay down on them. For the next four days she did not move from the cushions, lying quite still with her finger in her mouth. Nobody knew what to do until Sir Robert Cecil, whose father had once had Elizabeth's door broken down when she was crazed with grief for Leicester, went up to her and said, 'Your Majesty, to content the people, you must go to bed.' But Elizabeth, even though she was dying, was still a queen: 'The word "must"', came her answer,

> is not to be used to princes. Little man, little man, if your father had lived ye durst not have said so; but ye know I must die and that makes thee so presumptuous.

Finally however, she had to acknowledge herself defeated, and allow them to carry her to bed.

They had to ask her about her successor. The account of what happened cannot be considered absolutely reliable, because it was put about in the reign of her successor King

James and was so obviously to his advantage, but nevertheless it does indeed seem in character that Elizabeth on her deathbed should have said to her council, as was reported, 'I tell you my seat hath been the seat of kings; I will have no rascal to succeed me; and who should succeed me but a king?' So James of Scotland it was.

The Archbishop of Canterbury came to pray beside her. He was old, too, and found it hard to kneel on the floor, but Elizabeth seemed to take pleasure in his presence and would not let him go, though she asked him not to say anything about her greatness as she had had enough of vanity in her life. He had to pray on until, late that night, the Queen fell asleep. Then, shortly after midnight on the morning of 24 March 1603, she died.

She had been bastardized by her father and lost her mother to the headsman's axe. She had begun her reign in an England torn by religious upheaval and threatened by foreign enemies, as a member of a dynasty with an insecure hold on the throne; she had survived rebellion and attempted invasion and had transmitted her kingdom safely to her successor. She had ended her life revered almost as a goddess and within a few years of her death her reign was looked back upon as a golden period in English history. Above all, she had succeeded in turning her most obvious weakness, her status as an unmarried woman, into her greatest strength, by means of the cult which, diffused throughout every aspect of the Elizabethan court, had transformed a Tudor princess into the Virgin Queen.

Selected Further Reading

I

There are numerous biographies available of Queen Elizabeth and of the members of her family. The following are merely some suggestions.

MARIE LOUISE BRUCE, *Anne Boleyn* (London: William Collins, 1972)

ELIZABETH JENKINS, *Elizabeth the Great* (London: Victor Gollancz, 1958; reprinted Granada, 1972)

ROBERT LACEY, *The Life and Times of Henry VIII* (London: Weidenfeld and Nicolson, 1972)

JASPER RIDLEY, *The Life and Times of Mary Tudor* (London: Weidenfeld and Nicolson, 1973)

RETHA M. WARNICKE, *The Rise and Fall of Anne Boleyn* (Cambridge: Cambridge University Press, 1989)

NEVILLE WILLIAMS, *Elizabeth I: Queen of England* (London: Weidenfeld and Nicolson, 1967)

———, *The Life and Times of Elizabeth I* (London: Weidenfeld and Nicolson, 1972)

———, *The Life and Times of Henry VII* (London: Weidenfeld and Nicolson, 1973)

———, *Henry VIII and his Court* (London: Weidenfeld and Nicolson, 1971)

II

For information on the cult of the Virgin Mary, MARINA WARNER, *Alone of All her Sex: The Myth and the Cult of the Virgin Mary* (London: Weidenfeld and Nicolson, 1976); for Elizabeth's relationship with the Earl of Leicester, ELIZABETH JENKINS, *Elizabeth and Leicester* (London: Victor Gollancz, 1961); for Mary, Queen of Scots, one amongst many biographies is ANTONIA FRASER, *Mary, Queen of Scots* (London:

Weidenfeld and Nicolson, 1969); for Elizabeth's appearance and wardrobe, ROY STRONG AND JULIA TREVELYAN OMAN, *Elizabeth R* (London: Secker and Warburg, 1971); for the cult of Elizabeth, ROY STRONG, *The Cult of Elizabeth* (London: Thames and Hudson, 1977).

III

BALDESSARE CASTIGLIONE, *The Courtier*, translated by George Bull (Harmondsworth: Penguin, 1967)

IV

For information on the Cecils, DAVID CECIL, *The Cecils of Hatfield House* (London: Constable, 1973); on Queen Elizabeth's Maids of Honour, VIOLET A. WILSON, *Queen Elizabeth's Maids of Honour* (London: The Bodley Head, 1922); on the courtiers, NEVILLE WILLIAMS, *All the Queen's Men* (London: Weidenfeld and Nicolson, 1972).

V

LYTTON STRACHEY, *Elizabeth and Essex* (London: Chatto and Windus, 1928; reprinted Oxford University Press, 1981)

VI

For information on the Queen's own residences, IAN DUNLOP, *Palaces and Progresses of Elizabeth I* (London: Jonathan Cape, 1962); on those of her courtiers, OLIVE COOK, *The English Country House* (London: Thames and Hudson, 1974), and MARK GIROUARD, *Life in the English Country House* (New Haven: Yale University Press, 1978; reprinted Harmondsworth: Penguin, 1980), and *Robert Smythson and the Elizabethan Country House* (New Haven: Yale University Press, 1983); on the Elizabethan garden, see ROY STRONG, *The Renaissance Garden in England* (London: Thames and Hudson, 1979), to which my own account is heavily indebted.

VII

For information on progresses in general, IAN DUNLOP, *Palaces and Progresses of Elizabeth I* (London: Jonathan Cape, 1962); on the Kenilworth entertainments, F. J. FURNIVALL (ed.), *Robert Laneham's Letter* (London: Chatto and Windus, 1907).

VIII

For information on Elizabethan banquets, PETER BREARS, *Food and Cooking in 16th Century Britain* (London: English Heritage, 1985), and LORNA SASS, *To the Queen's Taste* (London: John Murray, 1977); on tournaments, ALAN YOUNG, *Tudor and Jacobean Tournaments* (London: George Philip, 1987), to which my own account is heavily indebted.

IX

On Elizabeth in art, ROY STRONG, *The English Renaissance Miniature* (London: Thames and Hudson, 1983) and *Gloriana: The Portraits of Queen Elizabeth I* (London: Thames and Hudson, 1987), to which my own account is heavily indebted.

Index

188

DATE DUE

Printed
in USA